MAGICIAN

VS.

MULE

The Ultimate Guide to Lifestyle, Wealth, and Freedom

By

Mark Evans DM

www.DreamStartersPublishing.com and Deal Maker Publishing

Table of Contents

Dedication

To all the Mules out there –
I get it. I was in your shoes. I used to be working my ass off to the bone and not going anywhere fast. Stay strong. The magician inside of you is about to be unlocked!

To my parents Mark and Sandy –
You are truly great humans. I'm amazed to this day how much you did for the girls and I. You have always supported me and I sincerely thank you for that. I love you.

To my amazing wife Deena –
You keep the house a home while I'm smoking cigars, working on my crazy ideas, and writing these books. I love you.

To my amazing kids Mark III and Dria –
You two are my light in the day. I love you more than words could tell you and I want you to know how excited I am to say "good morning" every day and "good night I love you sweet dreams" every night. You two are amazing! I love you. Daddy loves you and wants you to know that pursing your dreams with passion and hard work is what life is about. Stay focused and enjoy the journey.

Remember the only way to lose is by quitting.

With that said, let the journey begin.

Foreword by Tim Bratz

I was honored to be asked to contribute to the book by telling my own "mule to magician" story, much of which is the direct result from Mark's mentorship over the past five years. This is the story of when everything shifted for me.

I got involved in real estate investing for the same reason a lot of people do -- to create residual and passive income. I wanted the lifestyle. I wanted freedom. I wanted the opportunity to do whatever I wanted, wherever I wanted, whenever I wanted, with whomever I wanted to do it with.

But like many real estate investors, I thought I had to stockpile a bunch of my own cash before I could buy and hold rental properties. So, I went to work doing transactional real estate investing, doing things like wholesaling and flipping. The problem was, I was trading my time for money. If I made money, I had to do it again to get paid again, and I was only one person. I was doing everything in my business -- from finding deals to raising money, to collecting rent, and even swinging a hammer. There was only so much I could accomplish in a period of 24 hours.

The colossal question in my mind was, "How do I go from being a solopreneur to building an actual business that can operate with or without me?" I had no idea. I didn't know what I didn't know. I didn't know what the process looked like, how to manage it, or even what the first step was. I was paralyzed.

In August 2014, I was running an ad on Craigslist for a package of properties in Cleveland, OH that I was wholesaling, when a guy named Mark Evans reached out to me about it. We hopped on a call to discuss the package, and quickly realized it

3

wouldn't be a fit for his business model. But we kept talking, and the conversation ran its course to discuss things like the "solopreneur" hurdle I was facing in my business.

What boggled my mind is that Mark was calling me from a golf course during a six-week honeymoon he was taking with his bride to Hawaii and Bora Bora. I wondered, "How is that humanly possible? Who the hell is this guy? What does he know that I don't know?"

By the end of the call, Mark mentioned a mastermind event he was hosting in a couple months once he returned from his trip. The dates didn't work out for me, but we agreed to keep in touch.

A few months went by, the dynamic of the wholesale package I was working had changed, and I was now looking to take down the portfolio myself, fix it up, and sell off the properties individually. I followed up with Mark about it, and without ever meeting in person, we decided to partner up. He wired $10,000 for earnest money to the title company without any documentation in place. Again, I thought, "Who does that? This guy is either crazy stupid, has blind faith in strangers, or has so much money it doesn't matter." I was mystified.

As we worked the deal over the holidays of 2014, Mark mentioned that he had another mastermind coming up in February 2015. I had a thousand things going on and was too busy working IN my business. I couldn't get away for three days, because my business would fall apart! Plus, it was $5,000 for a two-day event. Although 2014 was the first year I ever made six figures, $5k was a lot of money to spend on a two-day event. Could I afford it?

The reality is, I got drunk on New Year's Eve and realized I couldn't afford NOT to do it. If this guy can wire $10k

4

for a deal we are doing without knowing me, I needed to have the balls to wire $5k for something that may have the potential of getting me off the hamster wheel that I was stuck on. So, at 10:30pm on December 31st, 2014, I sent $5k to Mark via PayPal.

I showed up to Mark's mastermind in Las Vegas in February 2015. I was able to meet Mark and his COO, Peter, for the first time in person. There were only about a dozen entrepreneurs and real estate investors in the room, and over the next two days, we discussed how to go from "mule" to "magician." One by one, we'd go around to each person, and they'd discuss the biggest struggle that they were facing in their life or business at that time.

What I came to realize is that every business faces the same struggles... sales, marketing, accounting, finance, human resources, operations, etc. Every business has the same foundational elements that transcend the product or service it provides. It's why entrepreneurs who understand the BUSINESS element of business can succeed no matter what industry they're in.

For me, it was getting out of my own way. I didn't know how to build a team. I thought I had to have everything in place, and I didn't know what "everything" even was. In fact, I didn't know where "everything" even began. I told the group how I was banging my head against the wall, day-in and day-out, taking on 100% of the work, responsibility, headaches, and liability that came with running my one-man-show.

Know what happened? The collective brainpower and experience in the room had seen my problem 100 times before. I wasn't alone. They went through it themselves, and because they went through it, they were able to offer insights on how I

5

could push past that barrier in my business. It was almost too simple of an answer. I almost felt stupid because I overthought and overcomplicated the situation. But sometimes when you're so deep in the weeds, you can't see anything from that outside perspective. That outside perspective is integral for helping to create a path to take you from where you are to where you want to go.

The advice I received was simple: hire an assistant. An assistant would take all of the urgent-but-not-important tasks and non-revenue-generating tasks off my plate. This would allow me to double down on the things that actually made money for my business – finding sellers, finding buyers, finding money.

But how was I supposed to take on an assistant when I barely made $100k the year before? An assistant would cost me at least $36k per year in my town. The group said not to look at it that way. Instead, look at it as $3k per month. If I tried it for a couple months, and it didn't work out, I risked $6k... not $36k. Wow. Just the framing of that in my mind changed everything for me.

I got back to Cleveland and hired an assistant who could begin March 1st. I had a newfound time freedom, not only to spend time on the revenue-generating activities in my business, but also to spend more time with my family. Over the next 10 months, I generated 3X what I had the previous year, and netted nearly $400,000.

Over the next couple years, I became addicted to leveraging the efforts of others. Just don't over-hire when not needed, like I did. The #1 reason businesses go out of business is because of lack of cash flow. The #1 reason for lack of cash flow is too much overhead. Whenever an issue popped up in my business, I said, "No problem, I'll just hire someone to do it." Instead, I should have first looked at fixing the flaws in my processes and operating procedures.

Nonetheless, by plugging into more masterminds and surrounding myself with other "magicians," I was able to refine my operations and become a magician myself. After just 4 1/2 years of thinking like a "magician" instead of acting like a "mule," I was able to transition from flipping single-family houses into exclusively buying and holding apartment buildings for my own portfolio. Over the past 4 years, I've been able to acquire 3,207 rental units with a total portfolio value of $251M, grow my net worth to multiple 8-figures, create a 6-figure monthly residual income, and design a lifestyle that most people can only dream of.

So much of that success is due to the philosophies taught in this book. Don't take it lightly. The philosophy and mindset shift in these pages will change your life!

Introduction

Today I'm writing to you from Coeur' D'Alene, Idaho. Ever been there? It is a magnificent place with fresh air, an enticing lake for fishing, skiing, blue sky, and a relaxed pace that lets me sit back and allows my creativity to flow. Tomorrow I may continue my writing in Montauk, New York while on a work vacation with my family, and from there, my home in Shaker Heights, Ohio. Or, I might be hanging out with my family in Parkland, Florida, sleeping peacefully at an amazing property that Mark the MULE would never have dreamed existed until I discovered Mark the MAGICIAN. This discovery was so enlightening for me that I knew I had to share it with you.

I'm not some highfalutin city boy that grew up with a silver spoon in hand… no sir. I'm just a good ole boy from small-town Ohio, population 650. It's the kind of place where everyone knows everyone and everyone's business. We didn't have stoplights -- and hey -- we didn't even have police. Career choices were limited and less than romantic, to say the least. You had the exciting option of working at the paper mill, working in construction, or working a farm. If you shake someone's hand and they didn't have calluses, well, they were just plain lazy. Calluses were synonymous with hard work. If you didn't work hard, you were looked down on. It was that simple.

And yet, when I was a kid growing up in this town, I figured out that I could have my friends do the work and split the money. I'd get a job mowing lawns and then get my friend to do it. I would charge $20 for the job. Then give $10 to my friend and keep $10 for myself. Here's the kicker. I had about five or 10 jobs at any given time. So, while my friends were making $10 for one job, I was making $50 or $100. Cool, right? But, as you may have guessed, I didn't have any calluses on my hands, and that labeled me as "lazy." People would talk it up that I was always looking for a way to get out of working hard. The truth was, I wasn't afraid of working hard. I just thought that I could do more and make more, but without having to do the physical labor to accomplish it. I know now that I had the magician in me back then even though I hadn't discovered a name for it.

Magician behavior isn't taught. It is within us the day we enter this world. It's the mule behavior and mentality that is programmed into us. Look at how you were directed when you went to school. You were told when to arrive and when to go home. You were told to sit down, when to shut up, when to raise your hand to speak, and to not speak until spoken to. This mule programming continues into adulthood. You get a job and are expected to be on the clock from 9 to 5, or some 8-hour shift. Even when you finish early, you're required to stay put until it's time to punch out just so you can prove that you were there the whole time. This is just a continuation of mule programming. Sure, the calluses I had weren't on my hands. I was different, but they are there. They reside in my brain from the years of constant attempts to reprogram me into a mule.

You might be surprised to know that you see and hear about magicians all the time. People like Warren Buffet or Michael Jordan come to mind. Before I was a magician myself, it was always a mystery to me how someone like Michael Jordan seemed to be everywhere with new products coming out

9

every day. New shoes, sportswear, jeans, basketballs... you name it, he had his name on it. But I wondered, with all this going on and playing basketball too, how could he be getting all this work done? The answer was that he wasn't doing the work. He was using his magician skills to orchestrate the people and companies that created his products. Other people were doing the work, and he became very wealthy from behind-the-scenes. In short, he became a virtuoso of his brand by orchestrating others to facilitate it all.

Think about that for a moment... sounds pretty enticing, doesn't it? But don't think that it doesn't take work.

At the age of 41, I have many successful companies, and I have started many more that have failed. I want to share with you my insights into being a magician versus being a mule – it's the wisdom I wish someone had shared with me when I was a child. Seeing my parents and others around me struggle their whole lives is what inspired me to write this book. **Throughout the book I'll be sharing with you my own metamorphosis from mule to magician, as well as lessons I have learned**. You'll discover my philosophy on why we do what we do and open your eyes to what is now versus what your future could be.

I ask now that you open your mind and immerse yourself in this book so that you can learn from the powerful discoveries that I have made. Discoveries that I know will change how you look at work and elevate your life. And, if you can grasp even ONE of them and implement it, I am certain you'll reread this book many times over as you journey through your transformation from **MULE to MAGICIAN**.

Chapter One

From the Beginning

I grew up watching my family -- and pretty much everyone I knew -- struggle financially. I can remember waking up at 5:00 a.m. along with my sisters and parents to get ready for our day. While my parents were getting ready, my sisters and I would eat our cereal. Then my mom would come out of the bathroom wearing her nice dress suit and smelling of Aqua Net Hairspray. Man, I remember that smell… it makes me smile just writing it.

At that young age, I'd think -- wow -- my parents are such amazing and hard-working people!

Next, we'd hop in the car, half asleep, and head to the babysitter's, and the day would get on its way.

My parents would work all day, and around 5:00 p.m. they'd pick us up and bring us home. Mom would fix dinner after already working a long day, and we'd sit down to eat together. I would listen to her talk about her day, about how hard she worked, and how the company didn't really treat her right. She told us that they fired someone recently, and in addition to her current workload, they would be giving that person's responsibilities to her. So, although she would be working the load of two full-time jobs, she persevered. In her next breath, she would say how thankful she was to have a job, and that she would suck it up until they hired someone to take the other person's place.

Of course, that never happened because my mother was amazing. When the company found out what an amazing MULE they had, they just let her keep doing the job. The more she did, the more they added.

Why did they keep doing this? Well, my mom would always figure out a way to get the job done. It was like she was Superwoman! (She has always been Superwoman to me.) She could multi-task and keep everything going at the same time.

And if my mom was Superwoman, my dad was Superman. He still is. I've seen both my parents bust their asses for years, and they continue to do it today.

I believe that my mother truly liked her job. She was at the same company for years but was afraid to say NO to her bosses. She was always worried and afraid that they might think she couldn't do a job and toss her out. She had three kids at home she was responsible for, and there were bills to pay. It was a big deal.

It made me feel bad to watch this go on. It really did hurt; even as a little kid, it made an impression on me. I didn't know why at the time. I doubt I even understood what an "impression" was, I just knew that it felt bad.

I commend my parents though, for doing what they did. I sometimes wonder today what life might have been like if they had understood about the magician and the mule. Where would they be now? Would I have taken a different path? I realize that these are questions that can't be answered, but I wonder, nonetheless.

We have all seen people that have amazing things and think to ourselves, "Wow, that's nice. Maybe one day I can have them too." But as we get older and find ourselves working harder, yet not getting any closer to the things we want in life, we begin to think that those things are just not for us. We start to push our goals and dreams further away as we hide behind the day-to-day stuff, or at our worst, we just stop pushing for them at all.

What I know now is that it's not the dream that's the problem. It's how we think and view the priorities that aren't allowing us to unlock the right path. We are MULES to a system that's been teaching us to be just that our whole lives. The amazing thing for me is that I have discovered this unbelievable, and what seems to be a mysterious, power that I never hear anyone else talk about... the MAGICIAN!

Since then, I have built many companies and been blessed beyond belief. I have incredible team members within my companies that work very hard to accomplish our vision. I have a family that means the world to me... my beautiful wife Deena, my son Mark III, who is four now, and my little ray of sunshine, Dria, who is three months old. My parents and in-laws are sharing in our lives too. My family is the most important force in my world. They are the reason for my endless energy and drive, and are the reason I am who I am.

Look, I barely graduated high school, and I never went to college. It just wasn't in my DNA. I lived in this town where most go nowhere. It was a town where nobody seemed to get rich. And yes, not everyone wants riches (or so they say), but acquiring wealth was something that always enticed me.

When I was 18, I had this epiphany. I had been watching one of those infomercials on TV about getting into real estate and how much money you could make, and it struck a chord with me. I called the number and registered for the three-day seminar and went down to Florida. I spent three days listening to their presentations and watching everything going on around me. I observed how the presenters and audience were dressed. I looked at how they carried themselves and spoke. I absorbed everything going on.

They talked about selling real estate versus investing in property and presented the value of residual income. This was when I realized that I could do this. I could set myself up with residual income streams. I mean, I figured out that getting one payday was okay, but what you really wanted was to do was get into something that would continue to pay out on a regular basis. In other words, bring in the money consistently, not just one month, but every month. I completely saw the sense in this, but I had absolutely no clue as to how I would get started. Keep in mind, this was all before the internet was a big deal.

Then, as I was observing the room, I saw one individual step on stage and pull out his phone. He sat in front of the room and opened the newspaper to the real estate section and started calling each person to see if they were motivated to sale at a discount. Then he got one ... I was hooked! Well, I thought to myself, I can do that. **And that is what got me started on my path to where I am today.**

After I returned home from the seminar, I immediately got started. I was already in construction, and I had a good working knowledge of houses; what to look for and that sort of thing. I figured it this way: a house has value to someone -- easy-peasy! Real estate seemed a natural career for me, so I decided to give it a go. I didn't really have much to lose at that point, so I jumped in and became intentional. I methodically searched through newspapers and identified what I thought would be good opportunities. Then I got on the phone and started calling each one until I finally hit on a deal.

I did my first deal in 1996 at the age of 18, and I tell you, it was ugly! I mean, it was incredibly sloppy. I had no clue what I was doing, **but I did it with intent**. I intentionally showed up at the house, I listened to the seller, and then went out and found a buyer that was willing to pay me more than I had invested. Voila -- I put together my first deal.

Looking back, I honestly thought that I knew IT ALL after listening to that guy at the seminar. Find a house for sale. Find a buyer. Collect the check. Seemed so simple. Of course, I knew nothing, and when it came time for making up the contracts, I had even less of an idea what to do. I reasoned that was what lawyers were for, so I called one and had him handle it.

This is what a magician does. **He looks at the situation, identifies necessary resources, and then utilizes their talents to get the job done**.

I made around $15,000 on my first deal. This was with zero money and zero credit involved. It was more money than I had ever made in my life! And more importantly, it was the start of leaving Mark the mule behind and becoming Mark the magician.

BECOME THE MAGICIAN

Ask yourself why you picked up this book.

_____

_____

_____

Where are you right now in your life?

_____

_____

_____

Where do you want to get to?

_____

_____

_____

"You don't learn to walk by following rules. You learn by doing, and by falling over."

Richard Branson

Chapter Two

Get Curious!

Are you curious? I mean, curious about how things work or what makes people do what they do? Man, I am! None of us knows everything… well, except maybe Steven Hawking did. I know you've heard that old saying, "Curiosity killed the cat," and right now, I'm going to tell you that's bullshit!

Take me for example. I would say that I am an ultra-curious person. When I see someone with something that I want, I'm not afraid to get curious and start asking all kinds of questions like, "What do they do? How did they get it? Why did they do it?" For me, it's all about trying to understand everything I can about who that person is and what makes them do the things they do. Then I store all this information in my mind's filing cabinet because, perhaps not now, but someday, it will serve me. This is part of learning and growing.

I remember one time when I was about 14 or 15. My dad had a construction business, and I was out helping him with a job. I noticed this guy standing nearby, and he had a red Ferrari 308. I always liked cool cars, so I made my way over to the guy and introduced myself. He was a nice guy, very professional.

Now, I'm ultra-curious, right? I didn't just want to know about the car -- my intention was to get to know everything I could about this guy. So, I sat there with him in a one-on-one conversation for a while. For some reason, I felt very connected to him, and it seemed like he was truly listening to me. I was for sure listening to him! I observed how he walked and how he looked at me when he spoke. I looked at the clothes he was wearing and at his shoes. I wanted to know where he came from and what he did. I wanted to know how he decided what he wanted to do and what he did to get there. It was all very intentional. I asked him many questions, and you know what? That guy was very willing to indulge my curiosity.

Now a mule may have admired the guy's car, but it would likely have been from a distance. They would never have thought to go meet the guy and ask all these questions. The truth is, they wouldn't have seen any point to it. In their mind, nothing this guy had or did would impact what they were doing, nor would he have any influence on their success. That is such a short-sighted thought process. Everyone you meet will have an impact on you in some way... everyone!

I wanted to learn and understand as much as I could about this guy because I somehow knew that getting to know all about him would help me get the things I wanted in the future.

A mule lacks that intentional curiosity. Their tendency is to look at someone that has something they want and ignore it. They have no time to be curious because they are too busy trying to get things done. It would also require that they keep their eyes open to the things around them, and mules tend to stay focused only on the task at hand. It's a sort of tunnel vision. I think that mules are so deep into the game of whatever it is they're doing, that they don't have time to be curious and ask questions. In their mind, they are working hard, and that hard work pays off! It is this hard work that will bring them their success. The problem with that kind of thinking is that the mule will keep working harder and harder, and in the end, achieve little or no success.

The magician has an innate curiosity and knows that the more he can learn from others, the more successful he can become. But here's the funny thing -- most magicians I know are dumber than mules intellectually. You're laughing, but it's true. Magicians are typically the screw-ups in school. I can tell you because I was one of them. The thing is you don't have to be smart to be a magician. I see a lot of guys, myself included, that are definitely not the "definition of smart," yet, we're able to create and run successful businesses. That's because magicians have the ability to get creative and capitalize on something the mules tend to miss. So, when the magician sees someone that has something they want, they get curious. They are highly curious and observant individuals.

Curious people tend to be people of action. They are always open to what is going on around them. They are attracted to new things and open to new ideas and experiences. They have inquiring minds, and of course, inquiring minds want to know all there is to know. It is this mindset, this intentional curiosity, that shows them not *what is*, but *what is possible* to attain.

What you need to do if you want to walk the path of the magician is to stop downplaying your curiosity. Intentional curiosity is a mindset. It is something you develop and keep working at all the time. The mind of a curious person is always alive and on the move. The more curious you are, the more questions you will ask, and the more you will learn. As you learn more, you will start to see more. You'll begin to observe the things the mules are missing because their heads are always down. Intentional curiosity is one of the foundations of the magician.

BECOME THE MAGICIAN

I want you to go to a high-end restaurant or bar. Get a table where you can observe the whole space. Take a journal so you can write down the things you observe.

Watch the people:

Notice and write down where they are, in the bar or seated at a table?

Who are they with?

What are they wearing?

What are they drinking, eating?

How are they interacting with other people?

Is there a magician in the room?

Get curious… what questions would you ask that person?

Are you brave enough to go and strike up a conversation with him or her?

"Price is what you pay. Value is what you get."

Warren Buffett

23

Chapter Three

Be Intentional

I am a true believer that we only get one shot in life. Life is very, very short and precious, but I find that many, probably most, people don't understand this. They think that they're going to live forever, and the way they play (or don't play) says a lot about their philosophy.

My wife and children are the real drivers for me in all of this. I always know they are watching me. For example, when I'm working out, and I know that my son is observing me through the window, he's going to either see that his dad is pushing himself or he's just slacking off. If I even think I might want to quit, just knowing that he's there watching me keeps me going and pushing even harder. Why? Because he matters. I am not going to ever let him see me giving up or slacking off. Kids are smart, man! You can only get away with so much crap before they wake up and call bullshit! Just knowing that he's watching keeps me focused and honest in all my actions. It's what drives me to be intentional in everything that I do.

What do I mean by being intentional? Everything you say, do or act on should have a purpose. Everything you do, and all the choices you make should be meaningful. Even your smallest actions have relevance. It means being completely engaged in the present, and to constantly stay aware and not let our attention drift away from the task or tasks at hand.

When I was a kid, I always wore the same clothes. I had on the same shirts and the same shoes, week after week, month after month. This made me conscious of what the people around me had. If I saw someone that had more than me, I paid attention. I noticed what they were wearing and how they carried themselves. I would check out their hairstyle and shoes, and I'd look at who they were hanging around with. It was a natural thing for me, and I still do this today.

When I walk into a room, I immediately pay attention to what is going on around me. I watch how people are responding to the other people around them. Do they valet? Do they not valet? What are they driving? Are they standing or sitting? Even the music in the background is important.

The point is that I am always, always conscious of my environment, from the largest to the smallest of details.

This kind of conscious attention to what's going on around me has been at my core for as long as I can remember. I remember the days when I used to go to clubbing with my buddies, and they'd all just casually hang about the bar acting like maniacs. They'd puff themselves up with exaggerated stories designed to impress the ladies, but I was different... even then. I was always very intentional about how I handled myself. From how I would enter the club to the exact drink I would have. For example, I never entered from the front entrance. I routinely entered through the back door because I wanted people to notice me and think, "Who is this guy coming through the back door?" I was always aware that how I entered a room would make people notice me. I've often observed how other successful people use this tactic as well. Mules don't think of these things; I know because I used to be the mule, and I'm talking from experience here. Mules don't think about how making an entrance will have an impact on whether someone notices you or not.

The focus a mule puts on their actions is very different than the magicians. For instance, every money decision I ever made as a mule was strictly based on how much something cost. Which, by the way, is exactly the wrong way to look at things, because it's never about the price. It's about what you get back in return for the money you spend -- it's about value! I was all tied up in the mule mindset that says how much something cost was everything. I had to get so pissed off over busting my ass trying to make money and knowing I wasn't pulling in as much as I could be before I could make a change.

Mules are stubborn! To get out of that mindset, I had to stop being a cheap ass and start looking through the eyes of a MAGICIAN, not a MULE!

My lawn care guy is not the kid down the street. My lawn care guy is a professional, and I want to help him make his business grow. You're right -- I could get it cheaper, but that's the mule-to-mule way of thinking. See, the mule is always trying to get something for cheaper, right? He gets such an ego trip over it, that he brags about it! The magician wants quality and value for growth. I hear these mules all the time talking about how they are abundant thinkers, but their actions say that they are scarcity driven.

I truly believe that you typically get what you pay for. Just look around you. Cheap and bad work is usually very visible. You hire a cheap company to do your lawn, and it will look like it. They might show up on time, or they might not -- they are cheap for a reason!

Take a look at your neighbor's house and the cheap paint job they had done. I would be willing to bet that the guy even bragged to you about how little it cost him. Yet, if you look closely, you'll see that the paint is already bubbling up because the contractor took shortcuts. But hey, if you like to have conflict and deal with problems like these, (which you created yourself by being cheap), go for it. I can't see any good reason for that kind of thinking myself.

A magician understands value over price. Here's an example of what I'm talking about. My company just held a massive event. We spent more money than we'd ever spent on a single event ever. Why? Because it was vitally important that the guests in attendance had an impactful and unforgettable experience. We weren't looking at how much it was going to cost, instead, we focused on the return for our investment. From the music, to the temperature of the room, to the chairs they would sit in, and more, we set the tone of the event by creating an atmosphere that would enhance their experience. We created an event unlike anything they had ever experienced, with the goal of leaving a positive impression thought of our company. The success of that event and the value we receive from it far surpassed anything we'd ever cultivated before, and we would have missed the mark had we only focused on price.

A mule would never think this way. As I said, the mule would be worrying more about the cost rather than the return, and that would override his ability to understand the value to be gained. In his mind, we would be crazy to spend so much money on something that he felt no one really needed. So, here's what I say to that mule: if no one needed it, then it wouldn't exist.

My unique way of thinking started when I was young, and I sought opportunities to further my development. When I got out of high school, I turned my car into a mobile university. I listened to everything I could on how to be successful. I immersed myself in becoming a better person; I wanted to live to the next level.

From the beginning, I knew that I had to create my own life. It wasn't going to happen while hanging around a small town with limited income and nowhere to go. I never read a book until I was 18 years old. Why? Because they just didn't interest me. I couldn't see the value in fictional stories that someone made up, but when I got turned onto *Think and Grow Rich* by Napoleon Hill, I'd discovered my kind of book. Since then I've read about 6,000 books on becoming a better person, because that's my personal goal -- to always work toward bettering myself.

One method I use is to deliberately set the tone of each day. Seven days a week, I wake up at 4:44 a.m. Why 4:44 a.m.? I intentionally picked that number for no other reason than it's a memorable number. Think about it -- if I tell you that I get up at 4:00 a.m. every day, so what? So do a lot of people. But if I tell you that I get up at 4:44 a.m. every day, that's memorable. I guarantee you that in some conversation, later on, you'll be telling someone that you met this guy at the gym who gets up at 4:44 a.m. every morning.

I have made it my goal seven days a week to get up at 4:44 a.m. and head for the gym. Not five days a week, not four days a week, but seven days a week. I admit that some days it really sucks, and other days, I have been known to sleep in. I'm fighting that tendency all the time, but I keep score on myself. As I said, I'm always trying to better myself, so seven days a week I'm up and at the gym early.

Your intentions dictate your actions. I see the same guys at the gym day after day. Some are like me, most of them are executives that work for some corporate giant, and a few of them are even friends of mine. What I don't see are too many mules at the gym with us. The reason being, that mules have created all this work for themselves and they are burnt out. When they get out of work, the only thing they think about is going out with friends and hanging at a bar. Instead of designing their lives, they are escaping them with a lot of whining going on. They order a glass of wine or a beer and spend the evening complaining about their jobs and how crappy their life is.

It is paramount that you are aware and conscious of everything you do. You probably don't realize the importance of how people perceive you, but there is a whole lot of research out there on body language and the non-verbal cues we send and receive. We make subconscious and instantaneous decisions about others from the cues we get. From the way you dress, to the way walk, to the way you enter a room, and how you speak, these details will make a difference in whether you control a room… or are invisible.

When I go to an event, the way I enter a room is very calculated. I want people to take notice, and I want them to want to know who I am. So, I hire two or three nice looking ladies to enter the room for about half an hour before I get there. They work the room handing out my cards to everyone. Then,

enough to instill confidence. My buddy was like most folks in my town, stuck in the small-town mindset of "Why would they" and I just kept thinking "Why wouldn't they?" That's the million-dollar question we should all be asking ourselves when we go after something, "Why the hell wouldn't they give me the job and the money?"

You know, it never occurred to me that I wasn't going to make money. It was always in my plan even though I started out as a mule. The only person that sets limits for us is us. Most people say "no" and are looking for a way to say "yes." I say "yes," figuring out of way to say "no." It's a different mentality. I say "yes" to most everything, professionally speaking. That's the difference in mindset between the mule and the magician. The "can do" attitude versus the "can't do" attitude. The "why would they" versus the "why wouldn't they" way of thinking.

Fear causes us to be self-limiting. I find that there are a lot of people out there that are simply afraid to ask for what they want. It's all because they are afraid of rejection, and I think they are looking at it all wrong. The worst thing that can happen is someone will tell you "NO." But if you *never* ask the questions and *don't try*, the answer before you even start is already NO. The point is, if you ask and someone tells you "No," you are no worse off than you were already. But -- and this is big -- if they tell you "YES," another door just opened!

I think it was Yoda that coined the phrase, "Do or do not. There is no try." Makes good sense to me.

BECOME THE MAGICIAN

So, what are you afraid of? Is it a fear of rejection? A fear of failure? Even a fear of success?

_____

_____

_____

What is holding you back from something you want or need?

_____

_____

_____

What will be the worst thing that could happen if you just asked?

_____

_____

_____

"One of the greatest discoveries a man makes, one of his great surprises, is to find he can do what he was afraid he couldn't do."

Henry Ford

Chapter Five

Progress Over Perfection

The truth is that it's never been easier to become a magician. In today's world, you have access to so many tools, it's out of this world. There's the whole internet thing that includes social media, video publishing, podcasts, and such. You can create and publish your own video that can be seen all over the world in an instant. If it goes viral, it has the potential to be seen by millions of people… millions! Imagine impacting that many people with a video post – it blows my mind. Remember, I got my start using newspaper listings and a landline phone…

Today, because of our world-wide instant access to information, companies are challenged more than ever to quickly bring to market more product with better value in order to survive. It's no small task either. You've got to constantly be looking to improve.

In my businesses, I'm looking for progress and improvement, not perfection. To me, becoming better is so much more important than hitting the bull's eye every time. I'm constantly moving the needle -- ask anyone who works with me. They know that continuing to improve is way more important than getting it textbook, right? Because we all make mistakes, it's inevitable! I'm not going to fire someone just because they made a mistake, even if we lose a deal and it costs us. We're going to sit down and look at what went wrong, and we're going to analyze what messed up and figure out what we can learn from it. Then, we devise a plan to make damn sure we don't do it again in the future.

We forget that we mess up all the time in life. You don't have to browbeat someone who is a professional. In my experience they'll do a pretty good job of beating themselves up. In my opinion, the mistakes we make are our best lessons. Learning from them is what counts, so we don't make them again.

I beat myself up more than anybody else ever would. I put so much more weight on myself than the outside world ever would. The world can tell me I'm a loser, I'm fat, I'm ugly or whatever, but the only story I hold true to is my own. I'm the only one I believe, and I'm going to work harder than anyone to improve myself.

So, let's talk about magic and effort.

Magicians are amazing! This time, I'm talking about magicians and illusionists in the entertainment business, like Penn and Teller or David Copperfield. These guys work tirelessly to reinvent their acts in order to stay on top of their game and ahead of the competition. They need to improve their game and create more innovative experiences for their audiences all the time. This takes hours and hours, weeks, and even months of dedication, to create a trick or illusion. Once a trick or illusion is developed, they still have to spend hours rehearsing and perfecting it, and that includes having a plan in place if something goes wrong. Audiences have no realization of what actually goes into making this all come to fruition on the stage. All they see is an amazing show-stopping performance.

As Mark the mule, I used to do events, and because I was a mule, I perceived that I had to do everything myself in order for it to be a success. I did the marketing, sales, collected the money, booked the venue, and picked the menu. It didn't stop there, because I also ordered the books, created the slides, and wrapped it all up in a bow. I was tired! The thing is, despite all the work I was doing, I ended up having a lot less impact than I intended. I was working my tail off for minimal gain. That's when I started to realize that I needed to think bigger and outside the box. There were people along the way that wanted to help me, but I never took them on. Now was the time. I had to start thinking bigger so that I could share my vision with people who could help me execute.

Now I have an amazing executive assistant that helps me run the ship. We were also able to hire the best event planner, sound and audio team, and a great marketing company to help plan and promote our events. I work less now, and we impact more people. We have been more profitable than ever, and I get to do the thing I love most -- spend time with my family, while making the impact I always hoped for.

If that doesn't feel magical, I don't know what does.

BECOME THE MAGICIAN

Think about a project you are currently working on or how you go about your mule day.

Are you spending hours trying to perfect something? Why?

_____

_____

_____

What value will there be in spending extra hours and time on a project that is already good enough?

_____

_____

_____

What is your motivation?

_____

_____

_____

Are you looking for perfection?

_____

_____

_____

Are you looking for recognition for your efforts? From whom?

_____

_____

_____

Are you afraid of making a mistake?

_____

_____

_____

"Have no fear of perfection -- you'll never reach it."

Salvador Dali

Chapter Six

Social Circles

Who are you hanging out with? Jim Rohn said, "You are the average of the five people you spend the most time with." I don't think most people even grasp that concept, but it's so true. We are all influenced by the people we hang out with and bring into our circle; this is so important to understand. If you hang out with mules, you will remain stuck as a mule. If you hang out with magicians, you're more likely to become one.

I don't like hanging out with people who talk about nothing. They talk about how rough their day was, then some other guy tries to one-up them, as if they're in a competition to determine whose job or life is the crappiest. It's what I call the "King of the Dipshits" mentality, and they're seemingly proud of their shitty lives. I will tell you, there are a lot of King of the Dipshits out there, who think they'll be rewarded for having a shitty life. If you make this your mindset, and keep doing this over and over for the next 12 months, five years, or indefinitely, where is your life going to be?

Here's an exercise for you. Next time you go to an event or party, walk over to the mules and ask what they've been up to. I guarantee they will regale you with how much they have going on, how busy they are, with the same ole same old stuff. You know – another day another dollar. When they ask what's happening with you, you tell them that you're keeping it simple. Watch what happens to their face – it's as though they think you are a lazy ass doing nothing. They have no idea what to say, and you'll immediately pick it up through their facial expression. They simply have nothing to talk about. When you try this exercise, most of the time, the mule will halfway acknowledge your comment and then say something like, "That reminds me of blah, blah, blah..." They will still try to one-up you with what they just told you before they asked about you. It's crazy – just try this and watch how it works.

We all have shitty stuff happening -- don't I know it! But here's the trick, you can't let it overrun you and be the only thing to talk about in normal conversation every day of your life. The longer you stay in a circle that thrives on that mentality, the harder it's going to be for you to get out.

If you want to become successful, you have to move in the same circles as the people that have what you want. If getting rich is what you want, then you need to move in wealthy social circles. Like attracts like, so the company you keep is going to be a huge influence on the direction you move. The people you hang with are the biggest influence on who you become; I believe this to my core. Negativity is going to create more negativity, and positivity will attract positivity -- you can bank on it!

To become a magician, you have to break out of the circle of your mule friends and move into the magician's social circle. This is not easy, of course. It means you need to get out, get curious, and start connecting with people you're going to be uncomfortable around... for a time. Here's the thing: the magicians aren't sitting around complaining about their lives; they're constantly moving and evolving in a positive direction.

BECOME THE MAGICIAN

This is very simple: take a good look at your current social circle, and the people you surround yourself with regularly. Keep in mind, this could be your family and loved ones.

How are they impacting how you think and view things?

_____

_____

_____

Do you all hang around complaining about life and how difficult things are? Trying to one-up the other with stories of how hard you work on this or that and never get any peace?

_____

_____

_____

If you want to get out and become a magician, are you willing to make the break and cut ties with your mule friends and move to a circle of influencers?

_____

_____

_____

"Your personal philosophy is the greatest determining factor in how your life works out."

Jim Rohn

Go to www.MarkEvansDM.com/magician to Win a 1-on-1
Full Day Intensive with Mark Evans DM ($50,000 value)

Chapter Seven

Teach Your Children

Who are your kids hanging out with? I talk to my kids about the world very seriously from an early age, and I highly recommend you do the same. I am so serious about this that my kids are going to be homeschooled. They aren't going to some public school with a broken system run by thieving administrators and learning from burnt-out teachers. We will teach them to read and write and give them the necessary tools to make it in this world, but we will do it in a more advanced way.

This is one example of how being a magician isn't always the easiest, cheapest, or most convenient path, but magicians are focused on results.

Here's what I mean. Think about how many times your kid comes home with some lame history assignment from a textbook, assigned to an entire class full of kids. What do you think your kid is really getting out of this? Wouldn't it be superior if, instead of reading a textbook about Egypt or Rome, he or she gets to stand in front of the Sphinx, the pyramids, or the Coliseum first-hand? That's real learning. We know that experiencing life far surpasses reading and memorizing a book in a stuffy classroom. You become part of the experience that way, and that gives you a different perspective and understanding.

I would much rather show my kids the world. We are fortunate to have the lifestyle to allow them that, but we also want them to work hard to get to where they want to be in life. They can do anything they want; I don't really care. They can be in construction, become a dancer or singer, or an author -- whatever they want to do. I just want them to be the best they can at it, and they aren't going to learn this in a classroom.

I'm clearly passionate about this subject. So many people in our country are hyped up about stuff they don't really understand because they never get out of their own provincial towns. They are brainwashed with information from sources like our censored media that tell biased stories about what goes on here and in the rest of the world. The propaganda is unbelievable. My wife and I don't want our kids living that way, being influenced by internet hocus pocus and gibberish. We want the choices they make that influence their world to be based on real education and thought.

I don't know what my world would be like if I had stayed stuck as a mule in my small town. I do know that I would probably be frustrated and not know why. Think about the legacy you want to leave for your kids -- do you want to carry on and complain about the world and your concept of what it should be, or do you want to act?

I cherish my family and my kids, and love nothing more than hanging out with them. To this end, I'm going to admit that I'm not a sports guy. I think sports is just an escape for people, and it does nothing for me. I don't understand the attraction myself -- who thinks it's cool for a grown man to run around in tights and a jersey? I don't want to be the famous quarterback like Tom Brady, or the famous coach like Bill Belichick. Instead, the magician in me thinks about how to be the owner of the team like Bob Kraft with the Patriots. They all have their places, and I know where I want to be. Being with my kids is my recreation. I spend as much time with them as I can right now while they're young, because I know that when they reach ten or twelve years old, I'm going to be out of the picture for a while.

Here's the bottom line on what I want for my kids: I want to teach them to be a good person and a giver first. Also, dad is wealthy and they're not. Now that may sound somewhat harsh to you but here's the thing -- I don't want to steal my kids' drive and passion for anything they want to do with their future. I want them to work hard, because it's the best part of the journey. I want them to experience things and be present with what they're doing. For example, I don't allow my four-year-old to get on my cell phone. We as adults have problems with addiction to these things already, so why would we want to teach that at an early age?

I want to encourage them to succeed. They don't need finances for that, they need encouragement and grit. I want to be a leader to them.

Some of my best memories in my youth were hanging out with my dad and uncles at job sites. They'd give me the tools and let me have at it. Even though I'd smash and cut up my fingers, they taught me hard work. These memories are awesome for me, and I want my kids to understand what it is to work hard.

There are what I call "delusional worlds" all around us from the crazy super-rich to ultra-poor. We all live in different worlds and our environments. Our view of the world is predicated on whether we are looking at it from the perspective of the mule or the magician. The mule's world is small and focused on the things he's always known. The magician steps out into the world and experiences it, inspired by the endless possibilities of what it could be.

It's my responsibility to teach my children the ways of the magician from an early age. Who are you raising? Mules or magicians?

BECOME THE MAGICIAN

This is academic: we teach our children to be mules from the day they arrive in our world. Why?

_____

_____

_____

What is your philosophy on education?

_____

_____

_____

Think back in your life. Were there any standout kids that didn't conform?

_____

_____

_____

Were you one of them? Have you felt like you were different somehow?

_____

_____

_____

If you have kids, are they in the conventional school system?

_____

_____

_____

Is college their next option for what we call "higher learning"?

_____

_____

_____

If you had the opportunity to get them out and let them experience learning first-hand rather than in a classroom, would you do it?

_____

_____

_____

"Students learn more by watching than they do by listening."

Robert Kiyosaki

Chapter Eight

Impact and Giving Back

Impact and giving back are essentially synonymous. What do I mean by that? When you have the means, you have the ability to give back and create a massive impact.

It's easier to give back when you're a magician than when you're a mule. You have the means to do more for your community, your family, and everyone around you. Being wealthy is much better than being poor. I can't see where you could argue that. I know because I have been both, and I didn't like being poor. Don't get me wrong, I'm not saying that being wealthy is the end-all to everything, but it does take a lot of the stress off for sure. Being wealthy gives you the resources to do the things you want in life, and it provides you with opportunities to impact the world around you.

The truth is that mules are so stuck in their lives that they don't know about the world out there, just waiting for them. Heck, I'm still learning about new worlds that exist, like VIPs at Disney and other companies. There are worlds that exist that can streamline and buy back your time because that's what we're all doing.

In my life, giving back is an essential component. For me, giving is like a muscle. It's the legacy I want to leave when I go, especially for my kids. It doesn't take much, so even if you don't have a lot of money, you can still give back. Here's why - - if you don't give when you have fifty dollars, then you won't give when you have five thousand or five million. Start giving now; it's something we can all do today. Even if you can only give $10 or $20, you're still giving.

Any time my four-year-old son gets money, I teach him to at least give 10 percent of it to charity and 25 percent to his growth fund. Money management is a crucial life skill, and the only way to get more money is to understand what money is and how money works. I'm very conscious of my duty and obligation to give back. I think being a great steward of money and time is our responsibility.

Think about the folks around you. I've never understood people that spend money on the latest cell phone. I used a flip phone for years! I don't see sense in running out to buy a $1,000 phone just because it's the newest on the market when mine works perfectly fine, yet there are people I know without a dime to their name that have to have the latest smartphone. They always have the best shoes and the hottest clothes, all the while, their bank accounts are in the negative, and they're running up credit card bills with high interest. It's a crazy mentality, and the system that has been designed loves the mules -- it keeps you a mule forever.

It's clear that these people don't understand that money is a responsibility. They don't understand how it works and can't see the impact that their actions have on those around them. It's the kind of thing that drives me bananas!

When I transitioned to the magician, the people around me started to get it. My parents have become very proud of me on multiple levels. One is that I don't flaunt my money in front of others and don't waste it.

For my birthday party every year, I host a benefit. We invite around 150 people over and hold a charity auction for 30 minutes to raise awareness and money. I designate a charity, and instead of presents for myself, I ask for charitable donations as gifts instead of presents for myself; I have so much already. Last year we raised $90,000, and this year, I targeted $100,000, but we actually raised $151,000! People couldn't believe it!

How many of you out there are having birthday parties and doing nothing but partying? This is a great opportunity to give back, and it doesn't take a lot. Invite some friends and tell them you're donating to a charity instead. All the people in my circle that I invited to my birthday came through this year, and the Caring House Project, couldn't believe how much we raised in just 45 minutes.

It all comes down to leadership and responsibility -- I steward my time and constantly lead by example.

We all know that actions speak louder than words, and I proudly can say that I don't just talk the talk, I walk the talk. Then when, like the mule, I share my stories with my friends, it becomes a sort of one-upmanship, but it's for good. We are all competitive on some level just by human nature.

Think about how the mule operates, albeit in a negative way, to always try and one-up one another on how hard we work. When I share what I'm doing in my circle of friends, they want to be part of it and jump on board. Suddenly, we start uplifting each other to do more. That's what happens when you're in a circle of magicians.

Here's an example: we're not into Go Fund Me pages, but if we know there is someone that needs help, we post what we need to a select group of about 30 magicians that we think will help us accomplish the goal. Whatever we need, we raise, and it's amazing to see it in action.

Our latest gift was for the adoption of a kid. It was going to cost $5,000 for this adoption to happen, so I posted it, and my friends started coming in with $500, $1,000, and more. I even posted $5,000 myself. We actually ended up raising about $10,000 for this adoption.

This is what I mean by leading by example. I don't just talk about it, and I think that is the true difference in my ability to make an impact.

There's a lot of people giving themselves gold stars and patting themselves on the back out there but let me tell you that there are more talkers than doers. I think that is partly because it has become so much easier to start a business as an entrepreneur today. Then they go around talking about it, but they aren't truly a success. We've all heard them. There's this philosophy of "fake it 'til you make it" going around out there that drives me nuts.

I'll never forget when I was about 9 years old, and I saw a man on stage in front of hundreds of people, telling them that the best way to become successful is to fake it until you make it. I was like, what the hell is he talking about? Why would you do that? It made no sense to me. In fact, it's a lot of bullshit! Back then you might get away with it, but now with social media it's a lot harder because people will see through it and will call you out in a nano-second.

The fact is that results are what count. At the end of the day, my philosophy is always to be the one bringing things to fruition.

Whether you are a mule or the magician, you need to always be honest and genuine with people. The guy that tells me that he'd love to do this with me, but he just doesn't know how it works, is the guy I'm going to want to help. But the guy that thinks he's got it all figured out and knows everything already, well, I'm going to think, "No one knows everything – that's dangerous talk." I'm not going to be very helpful to that guy. When I realized that just being straight up with people would actually help me, I became a much better magician.

The magician has no ego from my experience. The mule is struggling every day, trying to make it and is filled with too much pride. Taking pride in your work is great, and I don't take anything away from that -- it is incredibly important. But there is a difference between taking pride in what you do and being prideful.

I also believe that sometimes good enough is good enough. When I was in construction, I knew a guy that could stretch a two-hour job into a 70-hour job, just because he had to perfect it. There was little gain there except for his ego, and it's all he talked about. He could one-up the other mules by telling them how long it took him to do the job and how perfect it was, when in reality, he could have completed the job well in the shorter time. Good enough was good enough. All the additional time he spent was wasted on doing extra work for no benefit, simply to boast about what he had done and feed his ego. At the end of the day, he caused himself to miss out on the important and good things in life, like being with his family and enjoying time together.

The magician is able to think about the bigger picture. The magician is an orchestrator and an influencer. He is able to utilize multiple resources to create and manage all areas of his business. Do you honestly think that Bill Gates or Warren Buffet are sitting around talking about how much harder one worked than the other? We all know the person that is calm and cool and getting things done -- that's the magician.

Magicians are always growing and expanding their reach. They're the ones on vacation, hosting events, donating and giving. This isn't what mules do, because they don't have time to accomplish these things. They are so focused on the security or ego boost that they get from working hard, that they never think to look around them. Don't get me wrong. There are amazing mules out there, and they are a big part of what makes the world go 'round, but their capacity to do things is limited to what they are focused on. If you want to be a magician, you're going to have to let go of that way of thinking.

Know this -- when you're a magician, the extent of what you can do, impact, and give back is unlimited!

BECOME THE MAGICIAN

Think about how you operate right now.

Is your ego driving you? Is it recognition you are seeking?

_____

_____

_____

Do you really want to step out and work on transitioning from mule to magician?

_____

_____

_____

What are you willing to do to accomplish this goal?

_____

_____

_____

"Although I don't have a prescription for what others should do, I know I have been very fortunate and feel a responsibility to give back to society in a very significant way."

Bill Gates

Chapter Nine

Finding Your Identity

There are always people out there who think, "That guy had some advantage, like wealthy parents or a college education from an Ivy League school. That's how he got where he is."

The thing is, I didn't have any of that. I came from a very small town where no one is wealthy -- certainly not my parents -- and I was not born with a silver spoon in my mouth. What I did have was great, hardworking, loving parents. I credit their parenting and my upbringing, as it helped me become who I am today. Because of life lessons I encountered early on, I believe that in many respects, I had it easier than the rich kid. Just think about this for a second. How many rich kids do you know, or have you heard of, that just don't make it in the world?

People who've become a success have typically -- not always -- but typically, done it on their own.

The truth is that when your dad is ultrarich, you perpetually compare yourself to him. It becomes an internal competition, creates a problem at a whole other level, and that's just not healthy.

Then there are the rich kids that get bailed out at every turn. You see stories about this all the time, such as celebrities' kids overdosing or getting into trouble. Why do you think that is? Well, I think it's because their parents are so focused on their own careers and building up their own egos that the kids are left behind, and they aren't being taught how to make it in the real world. If something happens, instead of teaching their kids to figure their own way out of it, they do the lazy thing and just bail them out... over and over again.

The man I am today knows so much more than the one who started this journey back in 1996. I dug deep, worked really hard, did it on my own, and I'm continuing to learn and build.

Where you put your effort and energy is where the results show. As an example, if you're going to the gym and not getting results, it's because you're not doing it right. What you need is to pay a personal trainer maybe $150 an hour to coach you so you can learn and get the results. If you're doing it yourself, you're probably not motivated enough to do those extra squats or crunches or even show up every day. But when you're paying a trainer $150 to be your coach, you've got motivation. Why? Because you've put value on it. If you have to pay someone a contracted $750 a week to be your trainer, you're going to show up with intention. You may not like it every day, but you will show. You know that this guy is going to collect whether you show up or put effort into it or not. As a result of understanding the value and being accountable, now you are more likely to obtain results.

At the end of the day, the amount of energy you put into anything is what you're going to get out of it.

I hire third-party companies to come in and audit my books with me. Why? Because they help me to grow and learn how to read profit and loss statements properly, because they are always evolving. When I'm paying this person $200 per hour to be there, you better believe that I'm paying attention.

My point is that when you're paying someone, it's going to get done at least 99% of the time. You don't want to let them down much less yourself. When I pay someone, I make a commitment to them. I don't want to let them down, and here's the honest truth -- I'm more embarrassed to let that person down than to let myself down.

For example, if you're attending a free event, you're not going to pay much attention to it. If instead, you spend $100 or $500, there's value in what you take away, so you're more apt to stay focused and get something out of it.

I truly believe in the age-old philosophy of, "What you put into something is what you will get out of something." It's another difference between the mule and the magician. The magician is willing to put in any amount of work or money in order to reach their goals.

At the end of the day, money is just a tool. I want to expedite results, and money helps me accomplish that. When I want to do something new, I call someone to pay for their experience and time to help me complete it with their unique skill set. I'm looking to collapse timelines to completion.

If I call a trainer and they say, "Hey man, come join me every Saturday, it's free." Guess what? I'm not going. Why would I want to work with a trainer who doesn't understand or respect their own value enough to charge me? Right off I'm thinking to myself, "How good can they be?" It's all about value.

I want people who understand money, their value, and time.

To me, it's all about these three things: money, value, and time. You can call them my holy trinity. It's possible that you are thinking, "This guy is just money hungry," but it's not about that. It's about time and how you're spending it.

If you're reading this book, you want more, and you're willing to buy the book and spend the time to learn. Time is the only commodity we can't get back. You can go broke and bankrupt and then make money again, but you cannot get time back.

Look at Steve Jobs for example. He had billions and billions of dollars, but at the end of the day, none of it mattered, and not one single cent could save him.

I go back to the problematic arrogance of human nature. We all think we have time; we think we are living forever. They can say what they want, but I'm not buying it. For me, yes, I want to get stupid f'ing rich. If someone has a problem with that, well I don't genuinely care, nor do I want to hang out with them. If you don't understand your own identity and drivers, nothing will happen. Nothing will change.

Truthfully, it's not just about me. I want everyone I roll with to get stinking rich too, and that includes my team members. I want them to buy the best houses and cars and have a huge investment pool. That's what I strive for every day!

Additionally, my kids are young self-directed IRA holders. I want to create a massive financial wealth legacy for them because that is my duty and responsibility. Why? Because

I know it can be done. The way I see it, if I don't do it, who will?

A lot of my family does not get this. Most of them just don't understand this concept, as much as I would like them to. We've tried to talk, but I can tell that we're in different places, and I'm at peace with it. At the end of the day, it's an opportunity for me. Although I grew up poor and lived in a trailer park until I was ten, I acknowledge I can't do anything about that, but I can do something today. With the information I have now, I can keep moving up.

Which direction do you choose to move in?

BECOME THE MAGICIAN

Nothing in life is free. Take a good look at what you really want. Be brutally honest with yourself.

Do you want to be stupid rich and an influencer?

_____

_____

_____

Or, is the mule in you so strong that you think that there is no way you're going to make the leap?

_____

_____

_____

"I had no idea that being your authentic self could make me as rich as I've become. If I had, I'd have done it a lot earlier."

Oprah Winfrey

71

Chapter Ten

Let Go of the Obstacles

I cannot overemphasize the desire I had to do something different with my life than spend it in small-town Ohio. I knew I had to get out town and move up in the world. So, in 1996, I made a bold move and signed up for a real estate event.

At the time, I had NO money. I mean I had zero in the bank. In fact, I owed people, had no credit, and had bills due the next week that I couldn't pay. When I attended the seminar, I did it on borrowed money; I put the cost on a credit card and took a leap of faith. When I think back, it was a herculean effort for me to break out and do this for myself. I didn't question it then, because I truly believed that my effort to do this was going to pay off!

What I see now is that a lot of people just don't want to put in the effort. People talk big and tell everyone about how hard they work, but they aren't willing to go all in no matter the cost to make it happen. I mean, there I was, leveraging money against my contracting business that I didn't even have yet. So, it was going to *have* to work for me. That's how much I was willing to put into this.

I went to the seminar and found myself sitting there with 65 other people. I remember exactly where I was sitting, third seat on the left, next to a 40-something woman named Connie, and the instructors were right in front of us.

As I looked around the room, I noticed that most of the audience members were older than I was. It's safe to say that I was the youngest in the room.

Russ picks up the phone on stage and made a phone call to a number he got out of the newspaper. On the other end was a woman who answered that said, "Yeah, I'm getting a divorce, and I'm done with this. I want to sell and get out now." He made it look that simple!

What I noticed after that, was that people fell into two camps. I saw something I could do, but the older people were saying that it was all staged. Meanwhile, I was thinking, "How could it be staged? We all saw it, and we all had access to the same newspaper." I was so green back then that I couldn't even entertain the idea that someone might stage something like this.

During the breaks, these same older people were at the bar chatting it up about what a scam it was and no way they were going to fall for it. They were all skewed thinking this is all a put-up job. I saw an opportunity while they saw an obstacle. While they were at the bar sipping cocktails, talking about how hard they worked, and prattling along about how it was all staged, I was outside making phone calls right then and there. That's how motivated I was and how much I needed for this to work for me. I needed money! I was eating cheese curls and Doritos in my room because I didn't have a nickel to spend. I was so excited to make this work, because I had no other options.

There is a big difference in how the mule and the magician view opportunities. The mule will attend an event like this, and he'll be open to anything that comes his way as long as it's free. He'll take all he can get from that. But if they are asking for money, the first thing he thinks is that it's a scam and they're just making money off him. When the magician goes to an event, he thinks, "How am I going to make this work for me? What are the opportunities?" That's the difference right there -- the magician understands the power of opportunity. The mule keeps inventing obstacles to avoid making an effort.

Many folks do magician activities and don't even know it. I'll give you an example.

Cars are a passion of mine, but I don't have the first clue about fixing them. All I know is that I hop in my car, turn the key, it starts running, and off I go! Then comes the day that it won't start… now what?

There are two types of people. The one who will pull out his phone, get on YouTube to ask why the car isn't working, then invest 10 or 12 hours of his life trying to figure it out and fix it. He then brags to his friends how HARD he worked figuring it out, but he saved $300. So, you're thinking -- wow -- the guy saved himself $300! The other guy will take out his phone, call for roadside assistance, have the car towed to a local repair shop, then go on about his day. He's a mule, but he's acting like a magician -- he just doesn't know it.

Here is another thing to think about. Where did the first guy come up with the idea that he saved $300? From YouTube? I would argue that he doesn't really know how much he saved.

He estimated only what he thought it would have cost him to fix his car. What he didn't factor in were the 10 to 12 hours he spent fixing it. As we know, hours are time, and not to be cliché, but time is money!

How you look at things is everything. Being successful is dependent upon your interpretation of what you see or hear. How you take the information you have and use, will set your course. If you're not ready to put in the effort, you'll keep being the mule and going about your business of working harder with little to no gain. If you're ready to step out and become a magician, you will take that information, absorb it, and run with it!

BECOME THE MAGICIAN

Get out and go to a seminar. Don't be afraid to invest $300 or $500 or more to do it. Just go do it.

Look around the room. How many people are wearing fancy clothes and shoes? How many are flashing the latest smartphone?

_____

_____

_____

How many do you think will leave and go right back to their current lives?

_____

_____

_____

How many of them do you think will try just enough and fail?

_____

_____

_____

Do you see any people in the room acting like magicians?

_____

_____

_____

What are they doing? How are they acting?

_____

_____

_____

What opportunities do you see for yourself?

_____

_____

_____

"Only those who dare to fail greatly can ever achieve greatly."

Robert Kennedy

Chapter Eleven

TOTS – Thoughts on Thoughts

Everything today is instant, right? If you want an answer, all you have to do is ask Google, and you've got the answer. If you want to buy something, you can either go to the store when they're open and get it, or you can order it at 10:00 p.m. and have it in your hands the next day. It's instant gratification, and I believe it has created a massive identity crisis in our world.

I hate structure, but to tell you the truth, I am structured because I thrive. I have certain things I do every morning before I start my day before anything else happens. As I explained earlier, I try to make it a daily habit to wake up by **4:44 a.m.** seven days a week. I then make my social media posts that include thoughts or questions to the world. (If you're not following me on Instagram, you can find me at @markevansdm.) After that, I do some thought time which can

79

include meditation or journaling for about half an hour, and then I'm off to meet my trainer at 6 a.m. After my workout, I call my father at 7 a.m. to say hello, and then drive home from the gym. When I return home, I work on projects like this book, or work on a podcast – essentially investing this time to brain power.

Admittedly, I used to do mule things like waking up and grabbing my phone to email, text, or scroll through social media. It really messes up the tone of my day to be honest.

My goal isn't to open up email or start chatting online with anyone until after 8 a.m. This is precious time for myself to get in my thoughts and let my inner magician expand. It is crucial to be conscious of the start of your day. What happens after this may get a little crazy, but I have set the tone and controlled what I could.

To be honest, I think social media is the crux of the problem for many of us. I think they've created this crazy bombardment of information that makes it so hard to decipher the truth from the fiction that's out there.

Social media has created a platform where people can invent and make themselves out to be whatever they want. If you're reading this, I want you to think about something. Have you ever thought about why you think the way you do? This is the Thought on Thoughts (TOTS) theory. The problem is that if you come up with an answer, and you find it doesn't serve you, how much attention are you going to pay to it?

Who you are as a person is attached to your ego. If you receive the answer that you need to change, but it means cutting out some friends or doing things differently, you're not going to want to pay attention to that. That's the mule's way of thinking.

The magician, on the other hand, is always willing to evolve because they are never quite satisfied with where they are. I never cared that I lived in a trailer park, I was still me and was happy. I knew that it was just a moment in time, and we could evolve. We had a roof over our heads, and my parents busted their tails to provide.

But now, life is different, and I'm never completely satisfied with where I am at any moment. You can have stuff, but stuff doesn't mean anything. When I strip it all away, I'm always going to be that same person underneath that keeps striving to do better. I'm always going to push myself harder and faster to keep moving toward my goals.

Why do we think like this? **You can never build a big business or a big life with a small mindset**. If all your thoughts and conversational behaviors are around a million dollars a year, you will never get there. Don't get it wrong. When I say mule, it doesn't mean you don't make money. Mules can make a lot of money. They can make a million dollars a year, but they're still a mule to the system. They're still in that structural rut, frustrated and wondering why they can't break out.

What they haven't figured out is how to be a magician.

Think on this for a minute. What happens when you discover you were wrong? What do you do? We are all driven by our egos, so, what goes on when you realize that all the things you've been doing were wrong? That's a huge question! I can tell you that I've been wrong many times -- so many times! What you have to do is to reign in your ego so that you can look at things objectively and openly without allowing your emotions to take over. Put things into perspective.

We've established several times in the book that I grew up in a small town, and I think you're starting to understand what that was like. When people had money, well, that was a bad thing because they must have done something bad to get it.

There were perceptions on work ethic and even on race. What was even worse was when I questioned it, because questioning brought it out into the light. It created a whole lot of problems for me because, since I didn't believe the same way, it somehow made them look bad. It was all perception. Nonetheless, they deflected it onto me and made me into the bad guy.

This might have upset a mule, but not a magician.

Honesty is always the best policy in my mind. In the end, I think that mules are not willing to admit they might be wrong because they might lose friends over it. We all need to take 100% responsibility for our lives, our families, and our world.

The magician is not afraid to take on responsibility. I see it like this: everyone in the world is eager to take responsibility for things when they're good, but the separation between the mule and magician comes out when things go wrong and are out of control. Mules typically cannot accept this and tend to sweep everything under the rug or start blaming everyone else for what is going on around them. All of the sudden, they realize that they can't get out of it. They've backed themselves into a corner that they can't get out of.

The magician sees taking responsibility as very freeing. It's liberating to wake up in the morning and admit to yourself that something is going to go wrong today. This method is much better than putting on the fake face and telling everyone that everything is totally great in your world. Anyone who tells me that things are perfect in their world, I don't trust. Nothing is perfect in anyone's world -- nothing! Not only are they lying to me, but they're also lying to themselves.

I think that everyone should have to own a company for a year to see how things really work. Not just be the working mule but having responsibility for everything that goes on from the smallest detail to the end-product. Why? Because when you own a company, you have to be real with yourself. You have to know how to talk to people and manage people. You have to understand the inner workings of what it takes to get your product out the door. Then you have to understand your product and how to get it in the hands of your target audience. You have to understand the financial ins and outs.

It's beneficial to see business through the magician's eyes. You learn how people work, and if you don't get real with yourself, you're not going to be in business very long. I encourage you to open your eyes and your mind, to see things from a new perspective -- the magician's perspective.

So much of what you will accomplish in life starts with getting your thoughts in order. Take time to schedule your day, so that *you* are a priority upon waking. When you allow time for peace, silence, for reflection, for journaling, and mediation, you will discover your inner magician. The world will throw chaos at you, but if you take control of your own thoughts and actions at the start of each day, that is where the true magic will begin.

BECOME THE MAGICIAN

Are you the same person you were five years ago?

_____

_____

_____

How have you changed?

_____

_____

_____

How have you stayed the same?

_____

_____

_____

"How bad do you want it?"

Gary Vaynerchuk

Chapter Twelve

Move with Purpose & Urgency

I am very forward, direct, and straight-up with people when I talk to them. I don't try to be politically correct or constantly smooth it all out. It's very important to me that my communication with others is very clear and they understand it fully.

I don't have time to worry about whether it hurts your poor little ego or if you aren't able to fully grasp the opportunities that I present. I'm not wasting my time spinning things so that you don't feel bad.

How much time do you spend crafting your words and actions to not upset others? Are you getting your message out in a timely fashion? Are you getting it out at all?

Here's a true story. I sent out a success video not long ago, and some guy on social media messaged me about it and said, "Hey, Mark. I just bought a property from your company and it's amazing!" I jumped on it and told him that was great! Then I asked him if he could please make a short video about how great his experience was and send it to me.

He shot me over the video, and I sent it to my team in a text. Only one person out of 15 got back to me. Granted, it was a Saturday, but even so. I'm the type of guy who lives in a state of urgency, and I expect everyone around me to be on it at all times. Since I know this about myself, I kind of cooled my jets and sat back to give folks a little time to respond... you know, a little grace period. Then I jumped on it.

I'll admit, in addition to identifying as a direct communicator, I'm also a smartass. A short time later, after my generous grace period, I texted everyone and said, "Hey, I'm glad to see that everyone loved this video as much as I did!"

I suddenly started getting messages back with a whole lot of excuses as to why they didn't see it right away. I was like, "I don't want to hear your excuses! I expect you to be on it! If you can't do a simple task that is about a celebration of what we're doing here, what else are you screwing off on?"

A lot of times folks are just thinking that it's no big deal, but it's always a big deal! If that's how you do one thing, it's how you do everything. This lack of a sense of urgency is rampant and a big deal.

Take pride in what you do. I don't care if you are the nanny, the janitor, or the high-powered executive. If you are an executive and you're late for a meeting, guess what -- I bet you're late for every meeting.

MAGICIAN VS. MULE

Don't make up excuses. If you leave on time and can't get there, leave earlier. Here's something that really kicks my ass -- we have members in our family that are chronically late for every event. It's so bad that we make jokes about telling them the time is an hour earlier so that they will get to the event on time. It's such bullshit!

Be on time and be respectful. When you don't make it to something on time, it tells me that you have no respect for my time, and my time is precious. I don't waste it on people that don't have pride in what they do, or don't feel a sense of urgency to be on time and get the job done.

When I was in high school, I worked the night shift as a warehouse helper at the company where my mom worked. In between truck loads, there was dead time. There was typically three hours between each run, and usually a big mess in the parking lot of paper to pick up after each load. To this day, because of that job, I still pick stuff up off the ground when I see it. Why not? It doesn't take but a second, and it means something to keep our world looking nice. It's about taking pride in the things around you that a lot of people seem to feel are insignificant, but they really aren't!

The mule is the guy just doing *his* job. He marks his time as he goes about his business, clocking in day in and day out. There's no sense of urgency to do more than he gets done in the time he's on the clock. At 5:00 p.m., he goes home, and at 9:00 a.m., he returns and picks up where he left off.

To him tomorrow will be the same as today. There is nothing that compels him to make things happen any sooner than he gets to them. His focus remains single-mindedly on the task at hand, nothing more, and this carries over into everything he does.

Do you see the difference between the two? The mule is shortsighted, mismanaging his time, his responsibilities, and only thinking of his immediate job, task, and world. The magician looks at the big picture, is on time, is deliberate, and can be in many places at once.

The magician is always on the move. It's in his nature to get things done so he can move on to the next and the next and the next! Magicians position themselves in front of opportunities. Rather than just looking for a single opportunity, it's constant. They put themselves in every room and talk with everyone. They know they need to be on time, show up, and keep the energy going. It fits in with my philosophy that life is short, and time is precious. Don't waste it. If you don't change the way you look at and do things, the opportunities are not going to come. If you have a job to do, do it with pride and get it done, and then get ready for some magic to follow.

BECOME THE MAGICIAN

I want you to make a list of what your typical day looks like. Be honest and put it all down, charting the hours that you wake up, go to the gym, work, and come home.

Are you just muling out your days?

_____

_____

_____

What is the difference between how the magician operates his day and the way you go about yours?

_____

_____

_____

"When you are bigger than your purpose, you have a career. When your purpose is bigger than you, you have a calling."

John C. Maxwell

Chapter Thirteen

You Have Value

So, everyone is big on the movie "The Secret," where they tell you that if you envision something, it will manifest and come to you. Perhaps the secret is really about making commitments to yourself and sticking to them. When that happens, then other things start coming into your life.

We've all felt the energy when we get new cars or new clothes. You start walking with a swag, your presence changes, and you see things differently. You see these things happening, and if you can create this environment every day, the world knows you're showing up!

This is how you create opportunities. I'm attracted to people that have nice belongings. We are all attracted to people that take care of themselves. I'm especially attracted to people who get things done, not because they have more money, but because I can see that they are succeeding in life.

I've slipped up on keeping myself healthy from time to time. You know what happens when you're out there traveling and living in and out of a suitcase -- you're exhausted from just keeping up with your own schedule. Perhaps you're in Florence, Italy and say to yourself, "You're never going to be here again, so enjoy the food and drink. Have a good time!"

We create these excuses in our heads just so we can make ourselves feel good about it. Afterward, when we start seeing the weight on the scale start to creep up, and our clothes don't fit, we feel really stupid and beat ourselves up over it.

I want you to move on. It's past the time for beating yourself up about it -- it's time for you to get yourself back in line and fix it.

What I've come to realize as I keep moving forward is that we're all fixers. We're all in this to try to fix things for other people. We all have that buddy we can turn to when we want to get into trouble when we're at home doing nothing. And we have that other buddy we can count on to be straight with us. There is also that person in our lives that's kind of a hybrid, who tends to walk the middle road with us. The problem is that sometimes we get stuck going down the middle. That's bad because life is usually pretty comfortable there, and that can lead us back to doing our mule thing again.

I became overweight and out of shape. I was traveling, my wife's family is Italian, so all we eat is pasta and pizza, and these were all the excuses I told myself in my head to justify my behavior. In reality, I had no excuse.

It is up to all of us to take responsibility for ourselves and our actions. When you look at it clearly, I have all the advantages: I can do what I want when I want; I can work out anytime; and I have access to personal chefs that keep me on track and healthy. That middle road is so inviting and so easy to walk, that I was letting myself get stuck there.

I don't seek balance because I don't believe that everything can be balanced at one time. I think things move a lot and evolve as we go; it's an evolution and always a learning process.

I'm an anxious guy with an urgency to get as much done in my life as possible because I know our time here is short. I'm 41 years old now, but I know that I'm going to be 81 in a second; that's assuming I make it that far. The best way to do that is for me to be my own steward, for myself and my family.

A simple way is to look at the difference between how the magician and the mule are playing the game. The mule is playing to protect their downside, but the magician is all in and playing to win. It's a different mindset.

I used to watch my bank account every day. I'd sit and watch my account go up a thousand, five thousand, etc., and to me, if it wasn't going up, I was losing. I'd be upset and frustrated.

That was Mark the mule.

When I became Mark the magician, I figured out that I could take $5,000, invest it into an employee/team member, then go out and make $25,000! This sounds like a no-brainer, but when you are running around with the scarcity-based mindset, you start to get emotional about money. I couldn't get out of my own way to do that for a very long time. Back then, I was constantly asking myself, "If my account was at $0, how would that make me feel?" But I'll tell you now, if you are looking at your bank account through your emotions (and how you will FEEL), then you are in big trouble.

It's about playing to win. People who are mules don't want to risk any amount -- $100 or $1,000 -- because they are so worried about the potential loss.

True story, I knew this guy who had only $2,000 in the bank. He came to me and told me he wanted to invest in real estate and asked me what he needed to do. I told him to take $500 and buy a specific development course, to which he replied, "No way, I can't afford that." When I saw him two days later, he was wearing a new $800 sweater, and it was clear that his priorities were misguided. So many people's priorities are out of whack. The shirt makes them feel alive, but that shirt is never going to be an investment. People like this are more interested in how they present themselves to the world than understanding themselves. They don't see the value. They are more interested in what the world thinks of them than being real.

I just don't think people see the value of investing in themselves. I think this comes directly from the college system simply from the way it was designed. College was designed for you to go into debt for $100k to land a $25k job. Seventy-six percent of the people that graduate from college don't even get the job that they went to college for. I think they just get so jaded with the whole concept that they give up.

People have stopped learning and I don't understand. It seems to me that the average mule quits learning at a certain age, but I didn't even start learning until I got out of school. I listen to podcasts, read books, and get my hands on anything I can learn from to help me continually move ahead.

I am all about the long term, whereas most mules are looking at the short term. When I got into real estate, I was earning a whopping $200 a month and people actually cringed at this. My real estate investments started compounding over time, and within 12 months, I was earning thousands. When I found myself making all this money, I started feeling guilty. It was real. I was questioning how I could make all this money when I didn't feel like I was even doing anything?

This phenomenon messes with your head. We create a problem around it and bring in our mule mentality to try to make us feel better about making all this money, but it's counterproductive.

Mules and magicians have different visions. The magician is thinking ahead. He thinks that he needs to make enough money to take care of his family, pay for future legacy wealth, and do all he wants to do, while the mule is thinking, "I just want to make enough money to pay next month's rent."

Look, there is a difference between feeding yourself, feeding your family, feeding a village, or feeding the world. Ask yourself what you're trying to do. Are you trying to feed yourself, or your family, or the world? Each individual choice comes with different visions and actions, so choose wisely.

BECOME THE MAGICIAN

What do you stand for?

_____

_____

_____

Are you willing to invest in yourself?

_____

_____

_____

What do you need to do to get there?

_____

_____

_____

What's the most you've ever invested in yourself outside of college?

_____

_____

_____

Go to www.MarkEvansDM.com/magician to Win a 1-on-1
Full Day Intensive with Mark Evans DM ($50,000 value)

"Rich people have small TVs and big libraries, and poor people have small libraries and big TVs."

Zig Ziglar

Go to www.MarkEvansDM.com/magician to Win a 1-on-1
Full Day Intensive with Mark Evans DM ($50,000 value)

Chapter Fourteen

Get Out of Your Own Way

Let's talk about the chicken and the egg. In this analogy, I'm going to donate a hundred grand, but on one condition -- first I have to have ten million in the bank. That is just never going to happen! If you're not a good giver in the beginning, you'll never be a big giver in the future. This is a muscle and must be worked on.

This principle also applies to business. If you can't understand how to lead people, hire them, and work with them to help you grow, you're never going to be good at it. Without these skills, there is a very high probability that your business will fail.

What I am saying here is that if your focus is always and only on the money, you're looking at it all wrong.

The magician is all about developing people and inspiring them to believe in and support your vision. I believe that it's my job to talk to people, to inspire, and guide them to really look at themselves and understand they are better than they think they are. I want them to become better than they think they can be. Make sense?

Mules are so deep in the trenches that they can't see out. They just see two walls day after day as they tunnel along. They keep digging and digging, but never anticipate or see what's ahead of them. Mules are just using a shovel when they could be using a track hoe that could do with one scoop, what they've been doing for years.

People stay stuck in their own rut. For example, do you want a hundred percent of one hundred thousand or do you want ten percent of one hundred million? It's a choice.

The next time you drive down the street, look around at all the complexes being built. These are being built by wealthy people that are forming strategic partnerships in order to leverage the unique capabilities and strength of each other. It's just like Michael Jordan partnering with Nike. Each entity benefits from the other's unique abilities that they bring to the table. Magicians use this because it works. They know that they can't do everything and be everywhere at the same time.

I want you to spot the difference. Just like how in the beginning of the chapter I said that you can't just focus on the money, you have to focus on the people instead, here is another difference in thinking that marks a magician from a mule.

Whereas the magician partners and outsources efforts, the mule wants to do and be everything. They create bottlenecks because they have to do it all, because it's their badge of honor. They will literally kill themselves to do everything. I know and understand this at my core, because I *was* that guy before I figured out how to be the magician. No one was ever going to be as good at getting things done as me, that was for sure! I'd grab all the leads, make all the calls, do the follow-up, make the schedule, box it all up, send it out, track the delivery, and do the follow-up surveys. I don't know about you, but it makes me tired just thinking about it now.

Why in the hell did I think I could do everything anyway? How can you be good if you're doing a hundred things all the time? You've heard the saying, Jack of all trades, master of none. You cannot possibly be good at everything; you just can't.

You may be good at employment, but lousy at execution. Take me for instance. I'm a very fast-action starter with things but am a terrible follow-through person. I hate the day-to-day tasks, but love sharing the vision with my team. If you were to put me in the day-to-day follow up, it wouldn't turn out well.

Albert Einstein wrote, "Everybody is a genius. But if you judge a fish by its ability to climb a tree, it will live its whole live believing that it is stupid." We all have our interests, our talents, and our strengths. If we run around trying to be the best at everything, we will fall short, exhaust ourselves in the process, and barely accomplish anything.

As a mule, you feel like you know everything at all times, and think you're always in control, but I think you're just deluding yourself. You can't possibly keep up with that -- no one can -- and at some point, you're going to self-destruct.

My first company was a seamless gutter company. It was all mine, and I hired some high school buddies to work with me. I didn't understand that I was thinking like a magician, but since I was 12 years old, I understood the power of leveraging people. We started bringing in money, and the funny thing was, my people were making more money than I was. Not what you were expecting to hear, right? I've now learned that this is often the case when you start a business.

Here's the truth. Often times, especially right out of the gate, your people are going to earn more than you. Hell, you'll be lucky if you even get anything sometimes. You'll be sitting there thinking, "I'm the one with the vision, taking the risk, and doing all this work. I am only bringing in $500 a week, and they're making $1,500 a week. I must be doing something wrong." Well, what you're doing is probably a hell of a lot right.

Here it is: you're lucky if you're even making anything at the start. You're building your team, and you're building a company, which is something that just doesn't happen overnight. You don't just have this great idea and -- poof -- now you have a company making piles of money. It takes smart work, hard work, and an understanding of how to leverage resources and opportunity.

There is a difference between just building a job and building a company. The magician builds the company, and they understand that they may not make anything in the beginning. The truth is, it's not unheard of for a great salesperson to make more than the CEO at the outset, especially in the beginning when the company is small. This is good! It's good because this guy is the one who's pounding the streets and working to bring in the business. He's got your vision, and he is out there helping you grow the company. You need to be patient and keep the bigger picture in front of you at all times. Realize that, over time, the money will come, and your money will massively increase as compared to what that individual is earning.

There is so much more to building a company than dollars in the beginning.

You're the CEO, you're building your company, and how do you now keep your employees busy? That was the question I asked myself when I first started out. Keep in mind that during that time, I was still thinking like the mule and doing all these things myself. I finally did realize that I needed help and hired an assistant. We had problems because Mark the mule was a micromanager. My employees were wasting a half an hour emailing back to me the details of what they had been doing for the last half hour. Real productive, right? NO! It was the wrong thing to do.

You need to learn to trust and understand that the people you hire are going to do the job. Does it always work out that way? No.

I had a lady recently that went out to find a second job because she wanted more money to do things, I guess. Anyway, she thought that she was capable of working two full-time jobs. That is not allowed in our company, so I had to deal with that. Another employee's dad had a heart attack, and he had to leave. That meant that everyone else had to jump in and take on his responsibilities so the job would get done. It's the nature of owning a business.

The role of the magician is to paint your vision as clearly as possible so that your employees feel as though they are part of it. It's about defining roles. If you paint the picture well and hire people that grasp your vision, there will be no need for you to direct and micromanage them every single moment. They will run with it. The mule doesn't even have a picture, and that is why they never get out.

BECOME THE MAGICIAN

What is your vision?

_____

_____

_____

Right now, can you identify five people that can help you to achieve it?

_____

_____

_____

"Success isn't just about what you accomplish in your life; it's about what you inspire others to do."

Unknown

Chapter Fifteen

Patience

Ah, patience. This is something I don't have a lot of. I'm trying to learn, but man, oh, man…

I recently started another business. It took a year and a half for me to find the right person to run the division. This is part of painting the picture and having the patience to define and fill the right role for your company. There are a lot of questions you need to ask in order to ensure you are hiring the right person to carry your vision. It can be insanely difficult and anxiety-provoking because, like me, you probably just want to get the damn thing going. Here's the thing, if you don't take your time and instead, just grasp at the first guy out there, the impact on your business could be devastating. It takes a lot of time to recover from what a bad hire can mess up.

You need to have the patience to paint the picture you want. For the position I was looking to hire, I painted a vision of just that person. How did I do that? Well, I knew that I wanted someone who was young, passionate, hungry, and ethical in their dealings. Honesty is always at the top of the list for me. As I began formulating this person, I could see how they would fit into the role I was trying to fill. I put this together and started putting it out to the Universe and having conversations. A year and a half later, I found the perfect individual to fill the role.

When you know exactly what you want, you start to visualize it. But I want to be clear here -- you don't have to focus on every single detail, you just need to have a clear understanding of your goal. A lot of times people get too caught up in the details thinking that's part of the vision, but the particulars can come later.

The way to look at it is like this: here's my ideal result and here's my picture of the ideal person to fill the role. How we get there is probably going to take us over, around, and under the bridge, but first, you have to define what you want.

Say you want a brand-new black Mercedes Benz. Everywhere you go, you're going to see black cars. Then you start plotting how you're going to get it and start asking questions. Where can I find one? Who has the best deal? Pretty soon, you will wake up with a new black Mercedes Benz in your driveway.

When I am looking to hire and fulfill a specific role in my company, I want the best talent I can find. My goal is to create an environment where people are in tune with my vision and enjoy what they do; people who want to come to work every day. Every company has a culture that is developed as part of the vision. The individuals you hire need to understand your vision and fit in with the culture of the company. It requires patience to find the right individual.

If a mule is hiring someone for a position, they are more often than not, caught up in all the little details. As a magician, you're going to focus on the end-goal and the person who can best help you complete your vision.

Once again, this all comes back to patience. I'm very urgent in the now but have also learned to become patient about the future. Don't use patience as an excuse to not execute the effort, instead, use it to perfect your methods and create your magic.

BECOME THE MAGICIAN

Realize that transitioning from mule to magician does not happen overnight.

Do you believe that you have the patience to see it through?

_____

_____

_____

How long are you willing to commit to your transformation?

_____

_____

_____

Most people give up on their dreams after five years of trying. Will you?

_____

_____

_____

"There is a powerful driving force inside every human being that, once unleashed, can make any vision, dream, or desire a reality."

Anthony Robbins

Chapter Sixteen

All In

I am always all in! If you're only half-way in, you're a thief. You're a thief to yourself, and you can even consider that you're a thief to your Higher Power if you will. I want you to look at it this way: you've been given a gift. Whoever it was, tapped you on the shoulder and said, "Hey, here it is. Now let's grow!" When you're only half-way in, you don't hear it. You don't initiate anything and just pussyfoot around with what you've always done. In essence, you're stealing from yourself.

I've never had a real job in my life. If I don't kill it, I don't eat, and I'm fine with that. Most people are chasing a paycheck, but I'm chasing a vision of where I want to be. I don't want you to get me wrong, though. Doing what I do and going out and starting a company is not for everyone. There are a whole lot of ups and downs that come with it. Eating like a king one day, and eating Ramen Noodles the next, is the nature of the beast. It may not be for you, although if that's the case, I'm not sure why you're reading this book.

The point of this chapter is that while the mule can continue to focus on his small corner of the planet, the magician has to be open to the bigger picture and be all in.

I'm all in with everything because I have to be. If I'm not, the food is not getting to the table. I'm all in with everything that is accessible to me. For example, I'm all in with physical health, I'm going to hire the best people, and I'm going to eat the best food. In my assessment, if you're not all in, you're stealing. You're stealing from yourself, from people who could help you in the industry, and worse – you're stealing from your future self and from your family.

If you have children and they were reading this book, would you want them to come to you and say, "Daddy, I'm a half-ass at baseball and football and basketball! Yay, me!" If it's me, I'm going to tell them to pick one, go all in, and become really good at it. There is no half-assing it in my world. Every minute has to count!

Being all in means removing the safety net. What do I mean by that? You don't have time to be hanging on to some job and build a business too. Believe it when I tell you that this will only allow you to stay comfortable where you are because the net is always going to be there to catch you. There is no sense of urgency to get things done, and there is no need to accelerate the process. With that kind of philosophy, you better believe that you will go nowhere fast! I'd say the majority of people have gone soft in the world today -- they're only half in with everything.

You need to be willing to drop the net and walk the high wire if you want to be a magician.

You can't be afraid of falling down, or of doing something wrong. You are absolutely going to make the wrong decision sometimes. I will guarantee you that. I'll also tell you about those guys who are going to be sitting out there analyzing your every move and pontificating on how you did this wrong, or that wrong. I call this "armchair business building." They have all the answers as to why something you did didn't work, but none of them are moving forward. They're just sitting on the fence watching you. Pay no attention to them as they are secretly your biggest fans.

If you hit rock bottom, think of it as a gift. You can learn from this. You take the lesson and use it to pick yourself up, give yourself a kick in the ass, and keep going. Food on the table, right?

Don't focus on everything that's wrong. If you do that, you're going to have a very long list. Instead, focus on what's right. Focus on what you can control and how you can grow. Focus on improving. There is always, always room for improvement. I'm not a plain-view guy at anything, I'm always all in.

Sometimes you're the windshield, and sometimes you're the bug. It all depends on how you look at it. Either way, if you're going to be a magician, you need to put yourself out there. Make your decisions, right or wrong, stick by them, and adjust when needed. You might look like an idiot to some or a freaking genius to others. I don't hold much weight on either side. If I look like a genius to some, then I'll acknowledge it. As I said, though, I don't put a lot of weight on that. If you start buying into your own headlines, you're going to start believing you're invincible, and that breeds complacency. To me, the people who are talking trash are people that have what I don't want. What they say means nothing to me, and a magician cannot afford that.

Here's an example of what can happen when you're not all in. In 2005, there was a person in my real estate business that was amazing. Unfortunately, I was micromanaging the heck out of her and only paid her an okay salary. I never offered to improve her skills or help her move forward. I just kept giving her more and more responsibility because she was so good. I was pushing her harder and trying to pay her less at the same time. The result? In 2007, she finally left me.

I was muling her out -- I had been trying to turn her into my own mule.

In my defense, this is what I had been taught my whole life. It's what we teach everyone -- how to be the mule! The idea is that when people work hard but are paid less, the company realizes better value. Not true, but that philosophy was so ingrained in me that it was how I really believed things worked. I do feel really bad about what happened to her. She was an amazing person and a great team member, and I inadvertently ran her out.

I clearly remember the day she left me. I was in New York City, and when I woke up in the morning I knew. I had this feeling that entrepreneurs can get because we're so connected to what we do. Sure enough, I opened up my computer to find her resignation letter there in my email.

This is the one thing I regret to this day. The truth is that I've learned from the experience, and it has helped me on my path to become the magician. Now I'm on a mission to create many more magicians.

As much as I would love to say it's been nothing but one success story after another, that isn't the case. Fortunately, I use everything to fuel my fire and establish my path for the future. There was a time when I left a company that I was starting because it just didn't seem right. There was something about it that didn't sit well, and I wasn't into it. I was pussyfooting around and only putting into about 10% of me into it. I had the money and resources, but I just didn't believe in the bigger picture. I felt like it might be a good money-making opportunity, but I didn't feel like I could live or die with this individual I was teaming up with.

I don't get into business just to make money. I'm in it to have an impact. The money will follow. I want to feel like 10 years from now, I will be sitting around on a yacht with everyone and thinking about how far we've made it. If I don't feel like that, I'm not all in.

If you're the mule, letting go of the safety net is not an option, right? Being a mule is all about playing it safe in the name of security. They are never going to be all in because they would have to give up control, which is too much of a risk. On the other hand, magicians have a very strong decision-making muscle. They aren't afraid to put themselves out there and take the lumps along the way. They see it as all part of the process.

If you want the opportunity to come your way, you need to show the world that you are committed and all in.

This book is all about building your life and financial well-being/ You can't do that on a part-time basis. I only partner with someone who is all in. If you needed a heart replacement today, would you be going to a part-time heart surgeon? You may be laughing at the absurdity of the analogy, but you get my point. This is about your life and your future. This is serious.

I'm not working with anybody part-time. If you want me to work with you and give you opportunity, you're going to have to show me you're committed and all in. Otherwise, I'm not wasting my time and I recommend you do the same.

BECOME THE MAGICIAN

Have you ever started something that didn't feel right?

_____

_____

_____

Have you ever continued to do something that you hated?

_____

_____

_____

What were the forces causing you to do something that wasn't reflective of who you were inside?

_____

_____

_____

Have you ever given 50% of your effort to anything and succeeded? What makes you think you can with your business? Will you ever allow that to happen again?

_____

_____

_____

ARE YOU ALL IN RIGHT NOW?

If the answer is yes, let's talk.

117

"Most people fail not because of a lack of desire but because of a lack of commitment."

Vince Lombardi

Chapter Seventeen

Marketing

Marketing is nothing more than storytelling to gain profits. You create a story to sell your product. Many entrepreneurs don't want to be the face of the business, and that's okay. There are several companies out there that have avatars as the face of their company, such as McDonald's Ronald McDonald, and even Mark Twain was a pen name. If you think about it, most celebrities don't use their real names, and you don't have to either. What's important is the story you're creating.

If you make cat food and you're going after little old ladies that love cats, pick a cat for your avatar. If it's dogs, or kids, or teenagers, pick your appropriate avatar, write a story that will connect you with them, and market it. Marketing isn't rocket science. But it is a trained skill that can make you many millions of dollars.

In my real estate business, we know the client we're going after needs to have at least a hundred grand to invest. To this end, we're not marketing in areas that can't provide us with that opportunity. If you don't have a hundred thousand liquid cash on the table, you're not a fit for us. This is about staying conscious of what you are trying to achieve and consistently looking at the bigger picture. When you establish your target audience, then you can work on creating a story to connect with them.

In marketing today, we have so many unbelievable options and ways to reach people. We have the internet, email, and social media. I can market on Facebook, Instagram, and YouTube. I can even create a blog that I update every day. The platforms are almost endless, but don't try to do them all, though. That never works because you'll have too much coming back at you all at once, so, pick one medium and stick with it.

In 2005 I realized the power of the internet. It was a huge ah-ha moment for me! I suddenly had the ability to reach so many people, and I can't even tell you the effect it had on my ability to grow my business. My backyard became the world. I went from being able to reach people in a 60-mile radius to casting out to the world. At the time, I had no idea just how big it would be, but it changed my direction forever.

Once I had the power of the internet at my fingertips, I spent $50,000 and set up an opt-in page on the web. This does one thing only -- it has a box to enter your name and email address, and a submit button. I posted a small ad offering a free downloadable report, and once they entered their email address, it was immediately sent to them.

This turned out to be the best thing I'd ever done for my company to date. It was really the start of the whole magician effect and brought me to a whole new level of understanding. I now had endless possibilities, because THE WORLD had become my market. Because I took a risk and invested fifty thousand dollars in an idea, a possibility if you will, my business started growing bigger than it ever had before. You're reading this today and thinking how easy it is to set up an opt-in page for a few bucks in a matter of minutes, but in 2005, not so much. It was time-intensive and very costly for something that we take for granted today.

Talk to a mule about marketing, and they're going to tell you that the best marketing is word of mouth. Look, word of mouth marketing is not dependable because it doesn't replicate the message consistently. I agree that it's a good thing and we all want it, but it's not a marketing channel – it's simply the outcome of an activity. That means you had to get it, do the work, provide the value and when all that's done, you hope that people tell their friends, who tell their friends, and so on. It's all based on the assumption that the product will take on a life of its own and propel itself out there.

There are effective ways to stimulate word of mouth marketing, take for example, sending gifts. We send a gift to every single person who buys a property from us. After the deal is completed, we send them a Bonsai money tree thanking them for doing business with us. The reason we send a tree instead of the usual candy or flower vase is that people don't throw away living trees or plants. They will toss out candy, cookies, vases, and other crap, but you're never going to see a living plant in their trash. The Bonsai is a living, breathing being with majestic foliage and a thick trunk at its base. I would argue that some people are going to superstitiously believe that this money tree will bring them more money, and the power of this is amazing!

Here's what else we do: we ask. We follow up with our customers, we ask if they would put together a short video for us sharing their experience. If they agree and send one in, we share it online. We also send it to our internal list and our team. In this way, we create excitement and momentum! I'll be honest with you though; I was not always good at this process.

I've invested millions of dollars in masterminds and mentor programs from marketing to real estate to leadership and what it all boils down to is that you have to market and sell your product. I don't care who you are -- if your product doesn't sell, you don't have a business! To sell your product you have to market it. Even the most well-known companies in the world like Coke or McDonalds, continue to market their product because they have to stay relevant. You have to keep selling, and it's all about staying in the game.

When I say sell, I don't mean you have to go knocking on doors or stand out on a car lot waiting for a bite. I myself completely dislike that kind of selling. There are many forms of selling, and in my companies, we do consultative selling. I know what we can offer, I want to know what you're looking for so I can see if you're a good fit. If we're a good fit, we can talk about solutions, and if not, I'll see if I can point you in the right direction. No matter your approach, you have to sell!

When I do my events, we do everything "Four Seasons style" as I like to call it. If an attendee asks me if we have something, and we don't, the answer is always YES, never no. Always anticipate the question -- this is what Four Seasons does so well. They know you're going to forget your sunscreen or Chapstick in the car, so when you come in without them, they've got them for you. They know in advance if it's your anniversary or a birthday and there will be a card thanking you for spending your special occasion with them along with a bottle of wine or champagne. Now you know that probably cost them $50, but it's worth it because I'll be spending a thousand a night to stay at their property. The result is that I then share the experience via word-of-mouth-style marketing with all of my friends. I tell them my story, and they ask where they can sign up. This is the value you get when you market correctly.

By comparison, when I was still Mark the mule, I was always worried about the cost. I'd be scanning all the hotel sites and looking for the cheapest deals. That's what mules do, right? They are always thinking more about how they can save money. I would get a $150 per night room someplace because I was only going to be sleeping there after all. Again, magicians are looking for value. In this case, you get what you pay for. If you stay at the $150 a night hotel, you'll probably get a free breakfast consisting of powdered eggs, bad sausage, and weak coffee as part of the deal. Mules perceive that as being a great deal, and they will talk it up with all their mule friends!

Here's a fun fact about mules and magicians when it comes to marketing. Mules think marketing is an expense and magicians view marketing as an investment. Marketing is never a cost if you know your numbers.

I remember in my company we had a couple bad months with revenue. I sat down with my bookkeeper and she mentioned that we needed to reduce some costs. I asked, "What are you proposing? The first thing she said was, "Line 22 is a big cost to the company. Marketing. It needs to be cut in half or cut off 100% until we get some more revenue in the door." Needless to say, she was let go the next day.

If you think marketing costs money you have a long road ahead of you .... I know because I used to think the same way. The best way to get more revenue is to market your product and get the sales.

Sometimes we sell without selling. For example, if anyone in my organization talks to a potential client who mentions that they just lost someone close to them, we stop the conversation. We let them know we understand that this is a tough time and we can pick up the conversation at a better time. Then we send them a $50 - $100 flower arrangement with condolences.

We do this at all of my companies, and call it Care 360. We treat every situation like it was our own grandmother or grandfather on the line. It basically tells clients that people come first, because in my organization, they do.

To be straight up with you, I never had core values, so to speak. I just didn't think they were important, and how wrong I was! It can be amazing to see this in action. Customers want to be associated with a company that cares about people, not just the product or service they're selling. It would blow your mind to know how many talented employees you can attract with a Care 360 philosophy. In today's world, people seem to care more about the impact of what you're doing than they do about the money. They want to know that they work for a caring company.

I've been giving for years behind the scenes, but Care 360 has really been a great separator for our company. It's built into all of my companies' culture wand always will be. It's all about leading by example, because you can't just talk the talk, you have to walk the talk. If someone is going through a tough time, you help them out.

Recently, one of my team members found out that her father was diagnosed with terminal cancer. We got her on a plane immediately and told her to spend time with him for as long as she could. Core values aren't something you just espouse on a company website, they're something you must live and bleed. This is the impact you can have on the world. It's immeasurable in my opinion. Remember, you cannot ever out-give the world.

When you're looking at marketing, don't forget that by weaving your core values in, you can attract quality talent and clients who are a great fit for your mission and vision. Use your values to market your products to the right people, and let the magic begin.

BECOME THE MAGICIAN

Describe the difference between how a mule views marketing versus a magician.

_____

_____

_____

_____

_____

_____

_____

_____

_____

_____

"I've learned that people will forget what you said, people will forget what you did, but people will never forget how you made them feel."

Maya Angelou

127

Chapter Eighteen

New and Improved

At the end of the day, if you're in business and your product isn't selling, then you have no product -- I don't care what it is. You could have the best product since sliced bread or the electric car, but if it isn't selling, what you're doing is completely pointless! You don't truly have a business, because no one, and I mean no one, cares how hard you worked on it. The marketplace doesn't care. If you haven't done your due diligence and gotten out there to market it, then no one will even know it exists. How do you think you're going to sell something that no one knows or cares about?

Don't believe me? What are the top products you use today? I'm talking toothpaste, deodorant, etc. No one knows the story behind your toothpaste or deodorant; there may be millions of hours that went into making those products, but nobody cares about that! These guys figured out how to get the product in front of you and sell it. Who doesn't want gleaming white teeth? You don't care about how the toothpaste was made, but damn, you do care about what it's going to do for you. You want to smile that Colgate smile, right?

When you go on a date, you don't care who developed that deodorant you're wearing or how they got it into the container. What you want is to know that you smell good and manly for the ladies! At the end of the day, these companies figured out how to get that product in front of you through basic product placement. They figured out how to sell it, established their metrics and numbers, and went big with it -- that's the magician!

Every single day, magicians are thinking about marketing their product and getting it out there. They aren't thinking about how many hours went into making it, because that has no value to the buyer. They don't think about getting something perfect before they try to move it.

We call this progress over perfection. Magicians are worried about progress, while mules are stuck on perfection. Perfection is unattainable and subjective, massively subjective.

An example is the mule who built his own shed. He'll say, "I spent hours building it, and it is perfection!" As a magician, I also have a shed, and it's also perfection, but I didn't spend any hours building it. I called someone to come and build it, and that's the magician versus the mule right there.

Listen, there's no right or wrong in this. It's how one looks at it. I think it comes back to ego, they're those people who get their recognition from telling other people how they're doing all this work and how hard they are working.

Magicians don't do that. I don't call you up to tell you how I'm killing myself trying to get something done. I don't spend hours telling 25 different people about what I had to do to make this cool shed. That, to me, is a big waste!

My conversations are very different from those of the mule. Magicians are thinking about their next move. They're always thinking about the moves inside the first move. It's about just moving. Meanwhile, the mule is only focusing on the outcomes. They don't care about where they are going, they just care about their accomplishments.

When people are complaining about their journey, that's just wasted energy. It's wasted because they are so centered on their problems, that they don't have the time to work out a solution.

Obstacles to magicians are lessons. We're not bragging about the interruptions and obstructions, instead, we're bragging about how much we learned that day. We're talking about how we made 180 deals that month and the one snagged us. For example, "I was moving along so fast that I got complacent and sloppy, so it got away from me. You know, I didn't follow my own procedures."

We're always learning from the things we go through. Meanwhile, there's the mule who's always whining that they just knew it wouldn't work or it was a scam from the start. One of my favorites is when I hear, "I'm just a loser." They aren't learning anything; they're just wasting time and energy making up excuses for their failures. I just want to shake them awake and say, "What are you talking about?'

When my team calls me on the phone, I tell them to give me the baby. I want them to get to the point. I want the data, not the drama.

I'm totally and passionately solution driven to the point that I don't care enough about the problems. I tend to oversimplify things because my brain is always saying, "Let's move and keep moving -- we have to make progress!" If not, we get caught in the cycle and we keep getting deeper and deeper in the hole.

As we've established, the mule continues to look at the same thing day after day, trying to figure out how they can make one thing better and better. Meanwhile, the magician is willing to put themselves out there and up on the stage, even though they are making mistakes, they are learning and improving. It's all about improving.

Think about all the products out there that come out as "New and Improved!" You see them on the shelves all the time -- shampoo, protein powder, nut milk, etc. They are "New and Improved" because they are always IMPROVING! You can't improve something that never makes it to market, right?

You have to be out there. Just like those products, you have to continue evolving.

BECOME THE MAGICIAN

Describe how a mule perceives marketing a product versus the magician?

_____

_____

_____

Are you a solution-driven person?

_____

_____

_____

What if you or someone you work with makes a mistake, what then?

_____

_____

_____

"Those who seek a better life must first become a better person."

Jim Rohn

Chapter Nineteen

Time

Magicians and mules look at time differently. Time is the biggest commodity that we all want more of. You can't get it back -- when it's gone, it's gone.

I'm never going to retire because I've just don't see the point. If you love what you do, why would you retire anyway? I don't know about you, but I want to live while I'm alive.

What do I mean by that? Retirement was designed for mules. It's something for them to look forward to at the end of 40 years of muling for some corporate entity who didn't give a crap about them in the first place. The trouble is that by the time you finally get there, you're too old and worn out to enjoy it, or your health is failing. I've seen so many people retire in my small town, but now they don't have the money or energy to do all the things they waited all those years to do. Or, right after they retired, they got sick with some old age disease -- it's not worth it!

Life happens to all of us. We get sick, or our spouses die, or our kids get into some shit we have to bail them out of. It's a given. So many things can happen.

I was a class A mule back in 2005. I will never forget the day that I was notified that my grandmother was ill, because in two weeks' time, she was gone. It ripped me to my core. This was a big shifting point for me because I was the quintessential ego-driven mule. I wanted a big car and house, and I got off on everyone calling me "boss" when I came into the room. I was totally ego-driven during that time, but the day my grandmother passed away, I went straight to my office and bawled my eyes out! That's when I understood that I had to change.

I had money and opportunity, but what I didn't have was time. I was working 16-hours a day, every day and I loved it. On October 8, 2005, I went to Deena, my girlfriend, now my wife, and told her that we needed to go somewhere and take a month-long vacation. At this point I had never traveled for a day let alone a month. We ended up going to South Beach and staying for a full month, and man -- that was so freeing! I suddenly realized that I could make things happen away from the company. I didn't have to be on-site all the time. I realized I could walk around freely and still work on the company from afar. After South Beach, we took off for a trip around the world. We didn't even have a house for two and a half years while we were traveling. Talk about feeling free!

This life lesson allowed me to understand the value of time. This is what the magician understands. I like to think of it as the Mules are always inside of this huge maze. They know there's a beginning and they know there is an end, but they don't know where it stops until they're right in front of it. Now the magician, he's the guy sitting on top of the maze looking down. He also sees point A and point B. Then he just plows through the three walls that will get him to point B quickly, and that's the difference. I don't think most mules realize they are in the system. They are so busy inside the walls of the maze doing their thing, they don't know their own trajectory

My grandmother's death had a profound impact on me, as she was the rock and the leader of the family. After being diagnosed with stage-four cancer by the doctor, she only had two weeks left, and time was up. That was an incredible transitioning point for me that completely changed my perception about what life and time are about. We should all be spending time having fun while we're young before we get too old to enjoy it.

If there was anyone who taught me this lesson, it was my Grandmother. When we discovered that she was going to die from stage 4 cancer in 2005, I wanted to tell her in person how much she meant to me. But since I am such an emotional guy, I just couldn't find a way to tell her everything that I held in my heart. Just the thought of sharing how much I loved her would cause me to tear up and to start babbling incoherently. Instead, I got a tape recorder, wrote out how I felt, then recorded it. I can remember that moment as if it were yesterday. We cried non-stop as the recording played. Sitting there, holding her hand tighter than ever before, and us both knowing that time wasn't on her side will live with me forever. She would pass a week or so later. It all happened so fast and that's why it was so important to be able to do that before she left this world. I didn't have to live with any regrets. She knew how I felt and that meant everything to me. Looking back, I can't describe how fortunate I was to have been able to spend that time with her. Without my grandmother, I can honestly say that I would not be the person I am today. She taught me so much about life -including *live with no regrets*. Thank you Grandma.

As you can tell, time is a big deal for me. I think mules live with a lot of regret for not having done the things they wanted to before time ran out. You see it all the time. A couple retires, and before they've had time to enjoy their "golden years" together, one of them gets sick or dies. Magicians fearlessly put all their cards on the table. Yes, there's going to be hardship and pain -- it all comes with the territory. What I don't want is to live with the regret that hadn't taken care of the people I love, and I didn't go out and experience everything available to me.

I'm not talking about regretting some statement you made to someone, or a speech that didn't go quite right. I'm talking about the whole of your life. I see mules do this all the time. They're always planning for some trip they're going to take with their family… someday. It's so far out that it's never going to happen. Why can't we do something now? It's wild to me that people don't just take that trip now. You don't even know if you'll be here by the time you get around to doing it, or if it will still be possible.

Now is the tine to ask yourself, why are you putting things so far out? Mules always seem to be saving for a rainy day. There's not much money in the savings because it always seems to be raining, right? But you've got the newest smartphone and those new Louis Vuitton shoes. All you're doing is giving yourself a temporary high from getting something new. It's become so addictive to have the latest and greatest that you can't even see what you're really doing. It's just another drug, that's the reality of it.

This magician transition isn't easy, it's a process. When I first went to South Beach for the month, I was having massive anxiety attacks and dry heaving often, but I was detoxifying the mule out of me and transitioning into the magician. It's not easy, but it's mandatory if you want to live to your fullest.

Time is the key factor here. Keep in mind how many years you've been muling yourself out ... it takes a lot of work to deprogram that behavior, so focus on the steps and get excited. In time you will start to see some wins because of the magician in you.

Carpe Diem! Seize the day! There is just too much should-a, would-a, could-a in our lives. Take the time now. My message to you right now is this: quit making excuses for not doing things and just go out and do them!

BECOME THE MAGICIAN

If this was the last year of your life, what would you do now that you've been putting off?

_____

_____

_____

When was the last time that you went on a vacation? Do you have your next one planned?

_____

_____

_____

Instead of buying material possessions for your loved ones, how about you gift them with memorable experiences instead? Where would you go and what would you do?

_____

_____

_____

"Time is the most valuable thing a man can spend."

Theophrastus

Chapter Twenty

Financial Freedom

The first time I realized that I could have financial freedom, it was a big, big moment! It was that very first "a ha" moment when things became so completely clear in my head that I was really on to something! It came, by the way, at the first company I ever started, which was my construction company. When that first check popped in, I was filled with confidence and thought, "Mark, you got this!" I realized then that if I could get one person to spend their money with me, I could get a hundred people to do the same.

The grind and the hustle is all bullshit! We've all met entrepreneurs that make $500k a year busting their ass. They have no life and are on their cell phones all the time. I used to look at these people making the $500k and think, "Yeah, they're living the dream!" I'll admit, $500k is nothing to sneeze at for sure, and most guys that are making that money think they've finally "made it." The only thing I can see though is the cost they are paying to make that $500k. The reality for the mule is that his top earning potential really is probably $500k to

$1M. He's not going to make more than that. If he wants to make more, he's going to have to become a magician. I've been asking myself for many, many years, if not now, when? If not me, then who? So, why not me?

I had a buddy that had a pretty big online business selling shelves. And man, he was the mule of mules! He did everything from transporting the stuff to picking up garbage, to managing the place, to running the ads, to setting up the photoshoots, to meeting people halfway across the state, to putting labels on boxes. Then, at the end of the day, he managed the inventory, imported goods and dealt with customs, scheduled employees, and finally assembled furniture, etc. He did it all, but he didn't do it well. How could he? He was doing all of this with no system and no help. Some days he'd gross $70k. Some days he'd take a hit and lose $10k. He became so entrenched in running the day-to-day operations of his company, that he could never focus on building it into a real business that he could grow and eventually sell.

You know, everyone that plays in the big leagues has employees. They hire people. I know this makes the mule cringe because it appears that it will cost money, and he may be right that it will initially require some outlay of cash. But the magician realizes that each person they hire has value…VALUE!

For example, if I hire an assistant and that person costs me $36,000 a year or roughly $3,000 a month, I may take a small hit to my bank account initially. This is where the mule would freak out and never do it again. What the magician sees is that he may have to take a small hit until the assistant is trained and starts to get some traction. Now they're taking stuff off your plate, allowing you to focus on more revenue-generating activities. You just bought yourself back the most valuable asset in the world, TIME, and all for a small outlay of $3,000 a month.

Three thousand dollars is an investment, not a cost. Do you think if you had 60 more hours a week to focus on profit-generating activities that you'd make more? You better believe it! It never stops. As you develop your magician's muscle, you realize that every person you hire is buying you back more time, freeing you to focus on the things that matter to YOU!

Stop the burn-out activities! So many people are chasing where they think they should be instead of focusing on where they're at and what they can sustain. If you're making $500k, be happy. That's damn fine money and a good start to being financially free. But if you want to grow and gain so much more, get your priorities in line and stop buying all the latest toys and clothes. Always upgrading and buying that shit just pushes you further away from financial freedom.

The mule never has enough... of anything! They spend more time complaining about what they don't have, and they never seem to make enough. That kind of negativity is what keeps them stuck where they are. If you spend all your time complaining about life, you're never going to get anywhere. You'll be stuck in your small world still complaining about it the day you leave this earth behind.

I was once very conscious of every dollar coming in and going out, but it got to the point where it was running my emotions and life. That was Mark the mule at work. Depending on whether my account balance was up or down, I was happy or sad. I finally stopped letting myself get carried away with small details and started focusing more on what I was securing in the long run. As a magician, I can no longer spend my time worrying about these details, because I have the big picture in mind.

love the right people; the people that want to grow and break out from the mule mindset and become a magician. These are the people who truly want the financial freedom to do what they want in life. I get so much satisfaction from helping those people and seeing them grow and thrive.

I'm working with a guy right now who's making a $100k a month, but he wants to grow that. He knows there's another level out there and he wants to reach it, so he's coming to me to see if what he's thinking is even real. Sometimes people come to someone like me just to get verification that they can really do this, and I'm happy to oblige.

The truth is that the very best investment you can make is in yourself. If you're coming to me, it's because you want a life rich with rewards and business growth. You realize that I have the expertise to help get you there.

I've taken my life from Mark the mule to Mark the magician. There have been lots of bumps along the way, and there will be more. It's called learning. You're going to have your own bumps and hurdles to get past. I don't profess to know everything, but I have learned so much throughout my journey that I can share with you. You've taken the time to read my book. And I absolutely thank you for that. You know that for me this is about helping you go from mule to magician. All you need to bring is your want and desire to grow.

BECOME THE MAGICIAN

Describe your idea of financial freedom. Is it mule- or magician-driven?

_____

_____

_____

What are you willing to sacrifice to get there?

_____

_____

_____

"Wealth is the ability to fully experience life."

Henry David Thoreau

Chapter Twenty-One

Magician Effect

Henry Ford used to say, "Give me any question, and I'll have an answer in a second." In other words, if he didn't know it, he'd assemble his team and have the answer immediately. That is a skilled move by a quintessential magician.

Let's look at a couple of modern-day magicians. Richard Branson is a British business magnate, investor, author and philanthropist, known for his Virgin group of companies. He had the balls, the vision, and he manifested it. He had to stick it out, and he won!

Jeff Bezos of Amazon is a machine. Like him or not, he's a beast who has changed the way that we buy products. More importantly, I don't know if most realize the impact that he's had on creating a massive marketplace where others can become magicians themselves. It's truly amazing what one can accomplish with a vision and relentless action in a lifetime.

The more I discovered about the magician effect, the more amazed I became! When I realized how the magician worked – wow – I was on it! As a magician, you're able to do more and you're able to do it differently.

I want to remind you, that like most of you, I was trained in the mule mindset. I once I felt I *had* to do it all myself. Just because I managed to do it *all*, didn't mean that I was able to do it *well*. I finally realized that I needed to change my way of thinking and remove both my ego and the mule mentality.

It started in my youth when I hired friends for my lawnmowing business, and I've continued to assemble talented teams to execute massive events. I'll give you a recent example.

Mark the mule used to host events and singlehandedly put together the entire production. In truth, it wasn't sustainable -- it was too much for one person and burnt me out quickly. As a result of the workload, I was only able to invite about 12 people.

I finally had an epiphany and realized that in order to share my vision with the right people, I needed to think on a larger scale, and I needed help.

Recently, Mark the magician hosted an event in Columbus, Ohio for 150 people. Guests came from all over the country to attend Deal-A-Thon 2.0 and I threw a huge party. I used the magician effect to put it all together: I had a team of people set up; I invited a special guest speaker; and then I rolled in and spoke for five hours over a two-day period. We served lunches, dinners, and threw a hell of a birthday bash that raised over $151,000 to build an entire village in Haiti.

Because I changed my methods, I increased my impact. This is the POWER OF THE MAGICIAN!

What once took me hours to do, is now completed in about 10 hours with the help of my global team. They're between 30 to 60 strong, and we have regular meetings with the marketing team and event planners. Yes, it costs money to do all these things, but I remind you to look at the big picture. I can pay someone $10k to plan an event, which means that I can be free to sell 50 more tickets at $2k per person. That is a fantastic return on investment, that only a magician can pull off.

When I realized I had folks who wanted to help me, it just clicked! I could put everyone together and impact *hundreds* of people at once without spending hours on the phone, burning myself out. This is a method I've realized that magicians have, known as One to Many. Mules tend to do this one-on-one – I know, because I myself did it for years.

Outside of events, what does my typical workday look like? People will call me and say, "I know you're busy, but..." Busy? Do you want to know the truth? I'm sitting out back and enjoying a cigar because as a magician, things are getting done. I've hired a trusted team who are helping my business flourish. The magician way of thinking and operating frees me to do other activities, like generating revenue, planning my next move, or simply enjoying the things I love.

I now take calculated steps in the things I do. I've learned to put my ego aside and rely on those with the expertise to get the job done. I don't have to micro-manage or worry, and -- this is even more important -- I get to make *them* look good! It's a win-win for everyone when we step out of our egos and start to work the magic of the magician.

Yes, I am busy, but I'm *orchestrating* rather than *doing it all*. Do you see the difference?

Now that you've read my book, it's time for you to get started on your journey. A favorite quote of mine is "The art is in the start." Transitioning to a magician involves a very different way of looking at and doing things. As I've pointed out, it goes against everything we're taught and feel in our bones. Are you ready?

Establish Your Why

I'd like you to first establish your *why*. What is your motivator in this change?

For me, the most important thing in life is the legacy that I leave my kids. They are my soul, and the reason that I do what I do. My kids are my greatest joy, and I know that my time with them is short. I also value traveling with my family as it presents teaching opportunities and unmatched memories. It's a gift to see and experience different countries and cultures first-hand. Because of the things I've accomplished as a magician, my wife, kids, and I can do it all together, first class.

I want my children to know that I was more than a mule, created a positive impact in the world, and spent time with my family. That, to me, is the coin of the realm and the reason we're here!

That is what motivated me to go from mule to MAGICIAN. What is your reason?

Farewell Your Inner Mule

You've grown up in a society since birth, where following the rules, keeping your head down, and working hard is the expected norm. Be prepared for these changes to feel counterintuitive to your previous training, education, beliefs, and to how your family and friends choose to live.

As a reminder, below are the **typical traits of the mule**, and I want you to recognize what beliefs, habits, thoughts, and actions you're "guilty" of. Now is the time to release them:

- Rule follower who won't rock the boat.
- Needs recognition for job completion.
- Has an internal fear of failure.
- Lacks curiosity.
- Keeps their head down.
- Tends to have tunnel vision, stays focused on tasks at hand.
- Price is everything – cheaper is better.
- Would rather whine about how hard their life is.
- Not committed to anything.
- Asks, "Why would they?"
- Can't-do attitudes.
- Self-limiting beliefs.
- Believes micromanaging equals success.
- Won't let others help.
- Wants all the credit at any cost.
- Brag to their peers about how hard life is for them.
- "King of the Dipshits" mentality.
- Languish in their own negativity.
- Sends kids to the classroom where they are taught to be mules.
- Ego- driven.
- Prideful versus having pride in what they do.
- Complains about lack of money, but buys the latest cell, has a new car, new shoes, etc.
- Always wants something for nothing.
- Doesn't understand that you will get out of something just as much as you are willing to put into it.

- Would rather brag about how much energy they spent to make something happen rather than pay to get it done quicker.
- Fear of making mistakes.
- Places blame.
- Deflects responsibility to others if something goes wrong.
- Always worried.
- Lacks a sense of urgency.
- Just marking time.
- Doesn't look up to see the opportunity.
- Short-term thinkers.
- Only worried about the next month's rent.
- Seeks balance.
- Never looks beyond today.
- Kills themselves to do it all.
- Creates bottle-necks due to micromanaging.
- Jack of all trades, master of none.
- Always caught up in the details.
- Wants it NOW not willing to wait.
- Causes more problems for themselves due to their impatience.

Embrace the Magician Within

If you're reading this book, I truly believe that you're ready for this change. Transitioning from mule to magician isn't something you can ease into; it requires a quick and massive action. Pull the trigger right now and boldly cut the mule out of your life! Seize this sense of urgency and grab the things you want. Remember, the clock is ticking, and the time is now.

Here is your **ultimate guide to essential magician traits.** It's time for you to develop a new identity that will provide massive impact in your life, and in the lives of those you love:

- Analyzes a situation.
- Identifies necessary resources.
- Utilizes their talents to get the job done.
- Curious mindset.
- Has a thirst for learning.
- Believes the more he learns, the more successful he will become.
- Person of action.
- Intentional and calculated in everything they do.
- Understands the importance of value over price.
- Honors commitment to themselves.
- Asks, "why wouldn't they?"
- Can-do attitudes.
- No limits.
- Sees the bigger picture.
- Utilizes all available resources.
- Recognizes the influence of their social circle.
- Understands Laws of Attraction – positive attracts positive.
- Relishes the experience.
- No ego – prefers to work behind the scenes.
- Believes in giving back.
- Understands the value of money, time, and resources.
- Recognizes that what you put into something is what you will get out of something.
- Respects value and people who value themselves.

MAGICIAN VS. MULE

- Takes 100% responsibility for his/her actions.
- Willing to learn and evolve.
- Never satisfied, always moving.
- Has a constant sense of urgency.
- Always on the move.
- Positions themselves in front of opportunities.
- Gets things done!
- Long-term thinkers.
- Has a vision – thinks ahead.
- Understands there is no balance, scales are always tipped to create action.
- Looks to the future.
- Able to paint their vision, so others feel a part of it.
- Creates loyalty.
- Trusts people to get the job done.
- Has the patience to wait for the right resources.
- Has a clear understanding of the goal.
- Doesn't get caught up in the little details.
- ALL IN!
- No excuses.
- Every minute counts, everything counts.
- Understands their target audience.
- Knows the value of their product.
- Willing to spend to get a return on investment.
- Keeps it fresh to stay relevant.
- Progress-minded.
- Always thinking about their next move.
- Time is short – you can't get it back.
- Live in the NOW!
- Know that if they wait, they will miss out.

- Understands investing in themselves will pay-off
- Knows that financial freedom comes at an initial cost
- Leadership mindset
- Steps out of his ego.
- Thinks BIG!

The Art is in the Start.

I've always felt my purpose in life is to help people, and I especially love helping people who want to help themselves.

I think self-awareness is paramount when it comes to success. You need to know who you are at every moment, and when you are ready for change. I'm talking real truth to yourself, even when you're bullshitting others, you know that you can't bullshit yourself.

When I look back at how I got my start, I have to thank my parents, first and foremost. I am still mesmerized by how they raised me and my two sisters. They were amazing and I will never forget all the hard work they did and sacrifices they made to give us food, shelter, and to teach us how to be considerate humans in this world. Without them being who they are, I wouldn't be here writing this to you today.

I suggest you be honest with yourself, your journey, and open your mind to a realm of possibilities every day. It's all right there in front of you, you just have to reach out, grab it, and commit to it.

Now is the time to create the life you want. Today is the day to invest in yourself, your family, your future, and to transition from mule to magician.

Remember, we aren't guaranteed tomorrow, and there is no time like the present. So, become the magician as fast as possible.

It's time. Let's get started.

www.MarkEvansDM.com/Magician

See you on the other side!

BECOME THE MAGICIAN

Ask yourself, what's getting in your way? What's keeping you from starting right now? (That answer, by the way, can be, and is probably YOU.) Now, write down ways to overcome this.

_____

_____

_____

_____

_____

_____

_____

_____

_____

_____

_____

_____

"Whatever your goal is, you will never succeed unless you let go of your fears and fly."

Richard Branson

158

Go to www.MarkEvansDM.com/magician to Win a 1-on-1
Full Day Intensive with Mark Evans DM ($50,000 value)

Thank you for reading my book!

For more content, my podcast, products, success stories, and to access my social media, visit

www.MarkEvansDM.com

Go to www.MarkEvansDM.com/magician to Win a 1-on-1
Full Day Intensive with Mark Evans DM ($50,000 value)

Made in the USA
Columbia, SC
23 June 2020